TIMBERLAKE WERTENBAKER

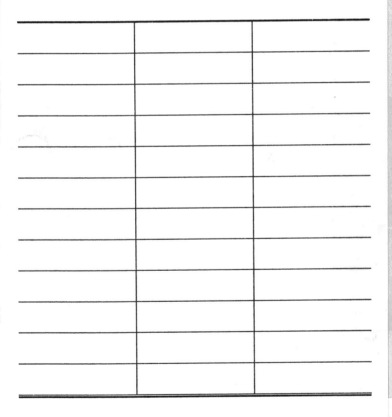
METHUEN DRAMA

Methuen Student Edition

First published in Great Britain in this edition 1995 by Methuen Drama

10

Methuen Publishing Limited
215 Vauxhall Bridge Road, London SW1V 1EJ

Peribo Pty Ltd, 58 Beaumont Road, Mount Kuring-Gai,
NSW 2080, Australia, ACN 002 273 761
(for Australia and New Zealand)

Methuen Publishing Limited Reg. No. 3543167

Photographs inside the book and on the front cover are from the 1988 Royal Court
production of *Our Country's Good* © John Haynes Front cover photograph:
Duckling and Harry (Alphonsia Emmanuel and Jim Broadbent)

The Letters from Joe White, Greg Stabler-Smith and Billy Reid are reprinted with
their kind permission

Photoset by Wilmaset Ltd, Birkenhead, Wirral
Printed and bound in Great Britain by Cox & Wyman Ltd, Reading, Berkshire

Contents

Thanks are due to Nesta Jones, Clare Naismith and
Timberlake Wertenbaker for their help and advice in the
preparation of this edition.

The works of Timberlake Wertenbaker

Timberlake Wertenbaker was Resident Writer, Shared Experience, 1983, and Royal Court Theatre, 1984–5.

Stage Works

This Is No Place for Tallulah Bankhead, 1978
The Third, 1980
Second Sentence, 1980
Case to Answer, 1980
Breaking Through, 1980
New Anatomies, 1981
Inside Out, 1982
Home Leave, 1982
Abel's Sister, 1984
The Grace of Mary Traverse, 1985, Plays and Players Most Promising Playwright Award
Our Country's Good, 1988, Olivier Play of the Year (1988), nominated for six Tonies and won the New York Drama Critics' Circle Award for best foreign play (1990)
The Love of the Nightingale, 1988, Eileen Anderson Award, 1989
Three Birds Alighting on a Field, 1991, won the Susan Smith Blackburn, Writers' Guild and London Critics' Circle Awards

Translations

False Admissions, 1983, from a play by Marivaux
Successful Strategies, 1983, from a play by Marivaux
Méphisto, 1986, adaptation of the play by Ariane Mnouchkine, from a novel by Klaus Mann
Pelléas and Mélisande, 1989, from a play by Maeterlinck

The Thebans, 1991, from the plays by Sophocles
The Way You Want Me, from a play by Pirandello
Hecuba, from the play by Euripides

Screenplays

The Children, 1992, from a novel by Edith Wharton
The Wings of the Dove, from the novel by Henry James

Television Plays

Do Not Disturb, 1991

Radio Plays

Léocadia, 1985, published in *Anouilh Plays: One*, 1987
La Dispute, 1987, from the play by Marivaux
Pelléas and Mélisande, 1989, from a play by Maeterlinck

Synopsis

Act One

Scene One: The Voyage Out
In the semi-dark hold of a convict ship bound for Australia, 1787, the convicts huddle together. On deck, Robert Sideway is being flogged. Second Lieutenant Ralph Clark counts the lashes. Sideway is untied and dumped with the rest of the convicts. John Wisehammer, John Arscott and Mary Brenham express the fear, hunger and despair that overwhelm them all.

Scene Two: A Lone Aboriginal Australian Describes the Arrival of the First Convict Fleet in Botany Bay on January 20, 1788
The Aborigine perceives the Fleet as floating from the sky – 'a dream that has lost its way' – and decides to keep his distance.

Scene Three: Punishment
Governor Arthur Phillip, Judge David Collins, Captain Watkin Tench, Midshipman Harry Brewer are shooting birds in Sydney Cove. They debate the punishment of hanging that has been passed on three convicts found guilty of stealing from the colony's stores. Phillip argues for a humane approach, believing this will encourage the convicts to change their ways in their new environment. Collins argues that the law must be upheld. Tench argues that the convicts are beyond redemption. Harry says the convicts have become immune to hangings and laugh at them – 'it is their theatre'. Phillip believes that 'real plays: fine language, sentiment' would be preferable.

Scene Four: The Loneliness of Men
In his tent at night Ralph Clark is composing and reciting

his journal to his wife in England, Betsey Alicia. We see a disturbed man who, in this new distant posting, is set against the convicts – especially the women – and is anxious for promotion. He is joined by Harry Brewer who comes to talk. Harry is a favourite of the Governor, having served him at sea for a long time. He feels some guilt about his past as an embezzler before he joined the navy, but his real anguish emerges as jealousy over Duckling, a convict whom he has saved from hanging and who now sleeps with him. Duckling has also slept with a marine, Handy Baker, who Harry has hanged for stealing food. Now Harry is haunted by Handy Baker who taunts him about Duckling. Ralph learns that the Governor is keen to educate the convicts, possibly by putting on a play involving them as actors. Having an interest in theatre, Ralph sees this as an opportunity to please the Governor and to get noticed. He asks Harry to recommend that he be involved in the play.

Scene Five: An Audition
The play is to proceed and is to be *The Recruiting Officer* by Farquhar. Ralph Clark is recruiting convicts to be in it. Meg Long (Shitty Meg) mistakes his new interest in women and offers to procure for him. She is dismissed. The pickpocket Robert Sideway is very enthusiastic about acting in a play and reviving his memories of London. Dabby Bryant brings on a timid Mary Brenham. Ralph is more interested in Mary, both as an actress for 'Sylvia' and as someone who can make copies of the text; he is doubtful about the forthright Dabby, who might play 'Rose'. The troublesome convict Liz Morden, intended for 'Melinda', snatches the play from Ralph and strides off saying 'I'll look at it and let you know'.

Scene Six: The Authorities Discuss the Merits of the Theatre
Governor Arthur Phillip and all the marine officers are present. The playwright describes the scene: 'It is late at night, the men have been drinking, tempers are high. They interrupt each other, overlap, make jokes under and

over the conversation but all engage in it with the passion for discourse and thought of eighteenth-century men.' The subject of debate is the play which Ralph timidly proposes to celebrate the King's birthday, on June 4th, and whether the convicts should be permitted to take part in it.

Most vehemently against the idea is Major Robbie Ross – 'You want this vice-ridden vermin to enjoy themselves?' he asks. The convicts, he believes, are there to be punished. He also claims that theatre can be disruptive of order and discipline – 'it teaches insubordination, disobedience, revolution'. In favour of the scheme is Governor Phillip who appreciates that the convicts must eventually 'help create a new society in this colony' and should therefore be educated and reformed. Captain Tench argues that the convicts should be made to work. The Reverend Johnson is concerned that the play should uphold Christian values. Ralph Clark claims that already, in rehearsal, some of the convicts have seemed to acquire a dignity and 'to lose some of their corruption'. The Governor allows the play to proceed.

Scene Seven: Harry and Duckling Go Rowing
In a rowing boat Duckling, morose and glowering, refuses to respond to Harry. He is suffering agonies of jealousy and fears that she is seeing someone else. Duckling hates being watched all the time – 'I need freedom sometimes, Harry'. Harry suggests she joins Lieutenant Clark's play, and she agrees.

Scene Eight: The Women Learn Their Lines
Dabby is pining for Devon when Mary enters to rehearse their lines in the play. Dabby knows that Ralph Clark is developing a strong personal interest in Mary, but Mary is still guilt-ridden over her forced relationship with a sailor on the long voyage from England. Mary resents Dabby's part in this – 'You sold me that first day so you and your husband could eat!' The two begin to rehearse and are joined by Liz Morden who demands to be included.

Friction between Liz and Dabby is averted when Ketch (James) Freeman, the hangman, appears. He learns of the play but the women unite against him in disgust and drive him off.

Scene Nine: Ralph Clark Tries to Kiss His Dear Wife's Picture

As midnight approaches Ralph is pacing his tent reciting his journal to his wife. He is obsessed with the sexuality of the women's camp. He is interrupted by Ketch. Ketch pleads justification for his past actions but is distressed that his position as hangman has set all the women against him. He sees a possible means of redemption and tells Ralph – 'I want to be an actor'.

Scene Ten: John Wisehammer and Mary Brenham Exchange Words

Mary is copying out the text of *The Recruiting Officer* and attracts the convict John Wisehammer whose liking for words leads them to an exchange on the sounds and meaning of words. The words are poignantly relevant to their situation.

Scene Eleven: The First Rehearsal

Ralph's formal meeting with his convict cast is disrupted by the animosities between them, and his first rehearsal is spoilt by the absence of Kable and Arscott. The 'asides' of Dabby Bryant indicate that these two have run away. The convicts display a range of misconceptions about acting which, despite their earnestness, results in high comedy. They are, however, silenced by the entrance of Captain Campbell and Major Ross who, in a fury, announces the escape of Arscott and Kable and the theft of food from the stores – 'and it's all because of your damned play'. Caesar, Wisehammer and Liz Morden are all implicated and threatened with dire punishment. The rehearsal is left in a shambles.

Act Two

Scene One: Visiting Hours
Liz, Wisehammer, Arscott and Caesar are all in chains. Liz
recounts her life story, explaining how she came to be
transported. Sentenced to death for stealing a watch, she
was granted the King's pardon and exiled. Wisehammer is
determined to return to England to proclaim his innocence
having been wrongly accused of stealing from a snuff shop.
Arscott has failed to escape because he was deceived into
buying what turned out to be a useless 'compass'. Sideway,
Mary and Duckling come to rehearse the play.

Scene Two: His Excellency Exhorts Ralph
Ralph tells the Governor that he wants to stop the
production because half of his cast are in chains and most
of his superior officers are against it. Governor Phillip
explains why he wants the play to succeed. The convicts
have to be reformed and their humanity restored because 'I
want to rule over responsible human beings, not tyrannise
over a group of animals'. Liz Morden becomes exemplary
in this respect. Recognising her as the lowest of the low,
the Governor has asked for her to be included in the play
in order to see whether kindness and good influence can
redeem her. Ralph is inspired to continue.

Scene Three: Harry Brewer Sees the Dead
Harry's hallucinations are uncontrollable. He is accused by
the voices of two that he has hanged, Handy Baker and
Thomas Barrett. Duckling tries to comfort him but he is
unable to trust her.

Scene Four: The Aborigine Muses on the Nature of Dreams
The Aborigine is disturbed by the continued presence of
the colonists. If they are ancestors from the Dreamtime,
how is he to relate to them?

Scene Five: The Second Rehearsal
Instructed by the Governor, Major Ross and Captain

Campbell bring the prisoners Wisehammer, Liz and Caesar to rehearse with Ralph, Mary, Dabby and Sideway. The presence of the officers inhibits the rehearsal and Ralph infuriates Ross with his assertion that 'there is a modesty attached to the process of creation which must be respected'. Ross humiliates Sideway, Dabby and Mary in front of the company. Sideway defiantly begins to act with Liz. Campbell is impressed. Ross orders the continuation of punishment to Arscott and his cries defeat any further attempt to rehearse.

Scene Six: The Science of Hanging
Ketch Freeman is dismayed at having to measure Liz for her hanging. Harry Brewer, still haunted by voices, orders him to get on with the business. Out of loyalty to Lieutenant Clark, Liz wants him to be told, after she has been hanged, that she did not steal any food. Harry suffers a stroke and collapses.

Scene Seven: The Meaning of Plays
The Aborigine continues to observe, not sure of what he is seeing and not knowing what to do.
   Ralph rehearses the convict actors but with little success. Personality clashes and ignorance of the conventions of eighteenth-century theatre continue to frustrate Ralph in his role as director, and the immediate threat to Liz Morden makes things worse. Wisehammer offers a newly written prologue which Ralph has doubts about. It is clear by now that Ralph and Wisehammer are in competition for Mary Brenham. The arrival of Ketch Freeman, who is to hang Liz, is too much even for Mary who has become dedicated to the play. Despite Ralph's plea that 'One has to transcend personal feelings in the theatre' he has to end the rehearsal.

Scene Eight: Duckling Makes Vows
At night, Harry is seriously ill. Duckling pleads with him to live, promising to answer all his needs, but Harry dies.

Scene Nine: A Love Scene
On the beach at night Mary is rehearsing her role as Sylvia.
She is joined by Ralph and the Plume/Sylvia relationship,
as they rehearse alone, is transmuted into their own. They
begin to undress.

Scene Ten: The Question of Liz ·
The officers debate the judgement of hanging on Liz
Morden. Collins is concerned that the guity verdict passed
on her is unsafe because the evidence is circumstantial and
she has refused to speak in her defence – 'because of the
convict code of honour. She doesn't want to beg for her
life'. Ross is certain that the convict is guilty. Liz is brought
on and both Ralph and Governor Phillip urge her to speak
– 'For the good of the colony . . . and of the play'. After a
long silence she does speak. The Governor looks forward
to seeing her perform in the play.

Scene Eleven: Backstage
The Aborigine has contracted smallpox and is now forced
to realise that the colonists he has been watching may not
be from the Dreamtime at all.
    The convict cast prepare to perform their play. They
rehearse their bow. Dabby is planning to escape back to
Devon and foresees both this triumph and the triumph of
the play. Wisehammer determines to settle in Australia and
be a writer. Sideway plans to start a theatre company in the
new land and the other convicts are eager to join him.
Black Caesar has gone missing, suffering stage-fright, but is
reclaimed by Arscott who threatens him with dire
consequences if he fails to perform. Wisehammer offers his
prologue to Ralph which states that

    True patriots all; for be it understood,
    We left our country for our country's good.

Ralph believes that this is 'too political' and tactfully
declines to use it. He thanks the actors for their work and
exhorts them to do their best. Arscott prepares to make his
entrance 'And to the triumphant music of Beethoven's *Fifth*

Symphony and the sound of applause and laughter from the First Fleet audience, the first Australian performance of *The Recruiting Officer* begins.'

Background

History and sources

Timberlake Wertenbaker wrote *Our Country's Good* in
1988 for a specific company of actors at the Royal Court
Theatre in London, where it was first presented in
conjunction with Farquhar's *The Recruiting Officer*. The
plays were directed by Max Stafford-Clark who has
explained:

> I first read Thomas Keneally's gripping novel, *The
> Playmaker*, at the same time as I was engaged on the
> Royal Court's bi-annual search for a classic. It's
> occasionally important for a theatre, primarily engaged in
> new writing, to measure its standards against work from
> the past. Like all the Royal Court's previous Artistic
> Directors, I also longed for a more permanent acting
> ensemble and the idea came of producing George
> Farquhar's brilliant comedy *The Recruiting Officer*,
> unproduced in London since William Gaskill's legendary
> 1963 production, together with a new play based on
> Keneally's novel.

The new play emerged from an initial intensive two-week
'workshop' in which writer and actors researched the
themes and the historical world of *The Playmaker*.
Although the starting point was Keneally's novel, the
research extended to investigate primary historical sources
and contemporary experience of military life, prison life
and the feelings of the severely oppressed. Much of the
background material is recorded under 'Further reading'
(p. xlvi) and details of the workshop method and
improvisations can be found in Stafford-Clark's book
Letters to George (Nick Hern Books, 1989). Obligatory
reading included Robert Hughes' history of transportation,

The Fatal Shore, and as a backdrop to their investigations, all the actors were preparing for their parts in the Farquhar play.

'The Playmaker'

Keneally's novel, drawing on many of the same sources that are used by Robert Hughes, was inspired, above all, by the idea of the play:

> There was an extraordinary poignancy in the fact that these folk whom Europe had rejected, the detritus of the European penal system, folk upon whom Europe never wanted to look again, should feel bound, even at the fiat of His Excellency the Governor, to reproduce here the great European religion of the theatre with its roots in rite, in dance and in mime. (*Sydney Morning Herald*, 30 May 1989)

Keneally makes the rehearsal of *The Recruiting Officer* the central narrative line of his novel, and invents the detail of Ralph Clark becoming the director, or 'manager', of the production. The convicts, who tend to be depersonalised and categorised as oppressed and tortured victims in Hughes' history, are here given individual life. The novelist imbues them with a sense of their depravity and with an ironic scepticism he recognises their baser instincts. The tone, here, is indicative:

> 'I have had great problems finding convicts who can act,' Ralph pleaded. 'Mainly the mad and stupid and the relentless villains have presented themselves, sniffing an advantage.' (p. 41)

Keneally establishes several of the relationships that are used by Timberlake Wertenbaker, and some that are not. The stories of Ralph Clark and Mary Brenham and Harry and Duckling, for example, are developed in *Our Country's Good* whereas the portrait of the eccentric Governor, Arthur Phillip (H.E. for His Excellency), and his tantalising relationship with the captured native, Arabanoo, is not.

Keneally's novel is dedicated to 'Arabanoo and his brethren, still dispossessed', which hints that the focus of the novel lies more towards the birth of the white Australian settlement than the redemptive power of theatre which is so strong a feature of *Our Country's Good*.

'The Fatal Shore'

Robert Hughes' book recounts in great detail the harrowing story of transportation. Between 1787 and 1868 Britain exiled 160,000 convicts to Australia, mostly never to return. Hughes explains why the convicts were sent, who they were, how they got to Australia and what they found there. He describes the development of the settlement around Sydney, in New South Wales, the horrors of punishment, and the mind-numbing atrocities associated with the further outposts – Macquarie Harbour and Norfolk Island – to which secondary offenders were sent. There is, throughout, a keen sense of the total subjugation of the convicts under this penal system. The book provides an historical background to *Our Country's Good*.

In particular the characters of the play are representative of the 'First Fleet' which arrived at Botany Bay after eight months at sea in January, 1788. The fleet of eleven vessels carried 1,030 people, including 548 male and 188 female convicts, under the command of Captain Arthur Phillip in his flagship *Sirius*. The convicts were relatively young (average age twenty-seven) and mostly guilty of petty theft. As Hughes points out, you could be hanged in England for stealing anything worth more than two pounds. These convicts were completely untrained and ill-equipped to start a colony in the new land.

Transportation was the answer to an extreme problem. The English prisons were full. Loss of the American colonies (Britain recognised the United States in 1783) meant that convicts could no longer be sent to work on plantations. The overflow from prisons, especially in

London, was incarcerated in hulks – old troop transports and men-o'-war – resting in the Thames and the Southern naval ports of England. This population was increasing by one thousand a year by 1790 and fear of typhus was real. Transportation allowed England to dump its 'criminal class' on the other side of the world, there to be forgotten, with the added advantage that returning ships could carry raw material home to equip the navy. Flax, for sails, and pine for ships' masts were the eighteenth-century equivalents of oil.

Most of the characters in *Our Country's Good* are mentioned by name in *The Fatal Shore*, and Hughes confirms that a production of *The Recruiting Officer* was performed by convicts to celebrate the King's birthday in 1789 (though not directed by Ralph Clark). Not least of the remarkable facts recounted in the book is that Dabby Bryant did escape back to England, after an initial 3,000-mile voyage in a stolen boat from Sydney to Timor with a small group of fellow convicts.

'The Recruiting Officer'
The play chosen to be performed by the convicts in *Our Country's Good* is *The Recruiting Officer* by George Farquhar (1677–1707). Farquhar was born in Londonderry, the son of a Protestant clergyman. He studied at Trinity College, Dublin, and was briefly an actor before moving to London to write plays. The success of *The Constant Couple* (1699) did not provide financial security, and a marriage to a widow with three children left him worse off. He secured a commission as a lieutenant in the Grenadiers and was himself a recruiting officer in Litchfield, the setting of his last play *The Beaux' Stratagem* (1707), and Shrewsbury, the setting of *The Recruiting Officer* (1706). This play was to become the most popular of the century, but Farquhar died in poverty at the age of thirty.

The convict characters in *Our Country's Good* become familiar with their roles in the Farquhar play, which is a constant point of reference throughout. The action

concerns the devious recruiting methods employed by
Captain Plume (to be played by Ralph Clark) and Sergeant
Kite (John Arscott) in Shrewsbury. They present a
formidable double-act – much too clever for the simple-
minded countrymen they aim to recruit. They approach
their women to get the men, and use Kite as a fortune-
teller to help their cause. The action also follows the
parallel romantic plots of Plume's wooing the spirited
Sylvia (Mary Brenham) – daughter to Justice Balance – and
his friend Worthy's (Robert Sideway) pursuit of the
haughty Melinda (Liz Morden). Both women have recently
inherited wealth which makes them the more desirable but
less available:

> **Worthy**   I can't forbear admiring the equality of our two
> fortunes: we loved two ladies, they met us halfway, and
> just as we were upon the point of leaping into their arms,
> fortune drops into their laps, pride possesses their hearts,
> a maggot fills their heads, madness takes 'em by the tails,
> they snort, kick up their heels, and away they run.
> **Plume**   And leave us here to mourn upon the shore – a
> couple of poor, melancholy monsters – what shall we do?
> (III. i. 1–8)

Both men have a rival in the form of the absurd Captain
Brazen (Wisehammer) – also a recruiting officer, and an
unlikely suitor to Melinda ('his impudence were a prodigy
were not his ignorance proportionable'). Sylvia, disguised
as Jack Wilful, escapes her father, intervenes between
Plume and the country wench Rose (Dabby Bryant), gets
herself arrested and is handed over to Plume as a recruit –
which is just what she wants. Worthy ends with Melinda –
(whose maid Lucy is to be played by Duckling) – and
Brazen is reconciled when Plume retires from the army to
marry Sylvia and hands him all his country recruits.

Farquhar's plays mark an advance on the cynical city-
based drama of his immediate post-Restoration
predecessors. Drawn from experience, *The Recruiting
Officer* is full of good-natured, genial realism. Honest in its
matter-of-fact depiction of the army and sexual behaviour,

the play does not employ irony and scorn so much as a
warm vigour. The convict cast, all except Dabby Bryant,
are completely taken over by their work on *The Recruiting
Officer*.

Not only the actors but very likely the original audience
of *Our Country's Good* would have been familiar with *The
Recruiting Officer* as both plays were performed in
conjunction (sometimes on the same day), so all the
references would readily be taken up. However Timberlake
Wertenbaker adds a further level of wit in her quotations
from the play, invariably making them directly relevant to
the convicts' situation and adding a meaning that could not
have been anticipated by George Farquhar.

Workshops at the Royal Court Theatre

The term 'workshop' can mean several things, and
frequently refers to a production that is not completely
'finished' – a 'work-in-progress' production which might be
seen by an audience. In the case of *Our Country's Good*
the term refers to the research method that was pioneered
by William Gaskill and Max Stafford-Clark with Joint Stock
Theatre Group in the 1970s. This involved the collaborative
exploration of theme and subject by the company,
including the writer who then went away to write a play on
his or her own. 'Although we intruded dangerously into the
writer's creative process, Joint Stock's success was in
knowing where to stop' (Max Stafford-Clark).

The Royal Court's workshop consisted of two main
elements – historical and contemporary research. Primary
sources included the journals of the original marine officers
(who provided material and stimulus for both Keneally and
Hughes), Henry Mayhew's histories of the London poor
(although these deal with a slightly later period), and
straightforward facts relating to London topography and
eighteenth-century theatre practice. The actors also visited
and interviewed various people who could inform them
about the military, prison life, the criminal mind, and the

experience of severe oppression (as reflected in the plays of
Andrea Dunbar). The actors, reporting back to the group,
might be quizzed or might dramatise their findings. The
visit to Wormwood Scrubs prison to see a performance of a
Howard Barker play (see p. xlix) by the inmates was
particularly influential. Sometimes incidents taken from
Keneally or Hughes were improvised on. However

> In the end, Timberlake was free to draw on all or none
> of these sources and what she has written should very
> much be seen as her own original work. (Max Stafford-
> Clark)

The workshop period was discussed in a dialogue between
Timberlake Wertenbaker and the actor Ron Cook (who
played Governor Arthur Phillip and John Wisehammer in
the first production). What is particularly instructive is the
balance that must be maintained by the actor who is
familiar with the source material and who is then presented
with a new role in a new play. This is part of the dialogue,
published in *The Listener* (November 1989):

Timberlake Wertenbaker People are always asking me
   about the workshops we did for *Our Country's Good.*
   What's in it for an actor?

Ron Cook I think it gives you a deeper understanding of
   the play and of the characters. The fact that it's a
   process of discovery, that you're not looking for
   something absolutely specific to your character, allows
   you to build up an incredible reservoir of information
   which you can tap into later in rehearsals. And you
   feel you've contributed a lot more to the play and to
   your character. What's in it for a writer?

Wertenbaker I suppose there are two things. The first is
   the shared imagination between actors and writers.
   When I've brought plays into rehearsals before, I've
   often felt a four-week rehearsal period just isn't long
   enough for actors to learn about the world of the play.
   But during the workshops of *Our Country's Good* we
   all learned about a world together. We had the same

references. It's also fun to write for specific actors. You always do write for actors, but when you're writing on your own you can feel bogged down; you can stop seeing it or hearing it. It's good to have the actors in front of you . . . What surprised and delighted me most was the ability of actors to be researchers.

Cook   It's the kind of work I enjoy. I always research a part anyway. I gather all the information, and then have a period of percolation – just leave it there, and hope things will come to the surface in rehearsals. I leave it to instinct.

Wertenbaker   The most exciting thing for me was the 'live' research, when you went out and talked to those people – the army officers, the ex-prisoners, the con-men. That was the major input to the play.

Cook   You're getting information first hand, it's not any sort of intellectual exercise: you just observe the way people act, their atmosphere. You *smell* that, and it's very important for an actor.

Wertenbaker   I loved it when the actors brought back these characters. When you interview someone yourself, especially if you're a writer and not a journalist, you're interacting with them, possibly influencing them. I found it enormously exciting when we sat round in a circle, and watched and talked to a character that someone had brought back.

But when you got the first draft, were you surprised that the characters were not what you had researched, but a character that had gone through the specific imagination of a writer?

Cook   You have to stop yourself from creating the character before the play is written.

Commentary

Structure and meaning

While telling the story of how the first transported convicts
came to produce a play, *Our Country's Good* also relates
personal stories and individual histories which broaden the
play's dialectic and enrich its meaning. Although set in the
past and dealing with an event that actually occurred, the
play is modern in that the central issues are immediately
relevant. Both writer and director (in 1988) were conscious
that the play deals with fundamental subjects. As
Timberlake Wertenbaker has said:

> It is a modern play. I'm trying to write about how people
> are treated, what it means to be brutalised, what it
> means to live without hope, and how theatre can be a
> humanising force. (*New York Times*, September 1990)

Stafford-Clark identified the main themes of the play as the
theatre's potential to change lives, the human ability to
transcend circumstances and the power of language. The
historical setting helps to clarify these matters, as the play
itself argues:

> **Dabby** Why can't we do a play about now?
> **Wisehammer** It doesn't matter when a play is set. It's
> better if it's set in the past, it's clearer. It's easier to
> understand Plume and Brazen than some of the officers
> we know here. (p. 74)

The island setting
Washed ashore in the vastness of Australia the convicts and
their custodians form 'a tiny colony' and as such a
microcosm of society. To a heightened extent the play is
able to examine social relationships based on power and on

sex in a situation where the established assumptions might be challenged. The island setting provides the possibility of a new beginning and the potential for Utopia. There is a tension throughout the play between longing and nostalgia for England, felt by everyone, and the growing realisation that here is a land of opportunity for all. Not everyone is converted. Ross remains embittered:

> This is a profligate prison for us all, it's a hellish hole we soldiers have been hauled to because they blame us for losing the war in America. This is a hateful, hary-scary, topsy-turvy outpost, this is not a civilisation. I hate this possumy place. (p. 81)

However the experience of 'civilisation' felt by the convicts, and reflected in their treatment, has little to recommend it. Governor Arthur Phillip has high ideals of a just society and acts towards its creation.

> **Collins**   You have been made Governor-in-Chief of a paradise of birds, Arthur.
> **Phillip**   And I hope not of a human hell, Davey. (p. 2)

Australian audiences of *Our Country's Good* have been acutely sensitive to this aspect of the play which they regard as being about them:

> It is an impressive and in places profoundly moving play which speaks to all Australians, whatever their country of origin. It is a palpable reminder to all of us that Australia was built on institutionalised injustice and barbarism, and on the scarred backs of men and women exiled from England for England's good. (Leonard Radic, *The Age*, 1989)

The characters of the play fall into two groups, neither of which is harmonious. The naval and marine officers have distinguishing characteristics which are established early on, and apart from Ralph Clark – who is directly influenced by working with the convicts on *The Recruiting Officer* – they change very little. Their dramatic function is to articulate differing views as to how the convicts should be treated.

The convicts are a more vivid group and the play is
essentially concerned with what happens to them under the
influence of working on their play. They begin as a broken,
brutalised and dispirited bunch who are united in their
subjugation but are shown to be much more viciously
antagonistic towards each other than the officers are.
Under the influence of their play they become a group,
sympathetic and supportive of each other. They begin
'alone, frightened, nameless' and end by recognising each
other's worth. The play provides an answer to Governor
Phillip's question – 'How do we know what humanity lies
hidden under the rags and filth of a mangled life?'

The displaced community parallels the experience of
those washed ashore on a different island in Shakespeare's
The Tempest. The stories that are told in *Our Country's
Good* find echoes in Gonzalo's words:

> in one voyage
> Did Claribel her husband find at Tunis,
> And Ferdinand, her brother, found a wife,
> Where he himself was lost, Prospero his dukedom
> In a poor isle, and all of us ourselves
> When no man was his own (V.i. 208–13)

Such is the transformation that we see acted out during the
play that Australia becomes the 'brave new world/That has
such people in't'.

The liberal experiment

The transformation in the morale of the convicts which is
fully demonstrated in the play's final scene is a vindication
of the Governor's liberal experiment. It is his idea that the
convicts put on a play, and he explains very clearly why he
wants them to do so:

> What is a statesman's responsibility? To ensure the rule
> of law. But the citizens must be taught to obey that law
> of their own will. I want to rule over responsible human
> beings, not tyrannise over a group of animals. I want
> there to be a contract between us . . . (p. 59)

He believes absolutely in the 'innate qualities of human beings'
which include intelligence, goodness and talent. In this he is
opposed by Captain Tench and Major Ross. Tench, an arch
pragmatist, believes the criminal tendency to be innate and
that the convicts would be better served learning to work
and be thrifty. Major Ross argues the extreme case that the
convicts – 'vice-ridden vermin' – are there to be punished,
and that as a group they are beyond the pale. Governor
Phillip cites the example of the Greeks and Rousseau in
support of his attempt to create a civilised society. As the
play proceeds we see the justification of his argument.

A similar social experiment is found in Shakespeare's
Measure for Measure where another benevolent dictator
tries to educate his society. Vienna has become
disrespectful of the law and vice is rampant. The Duke puts
a Draconian figure (Angelo) in charge in order to show the
people what happens when the law is flouted and then
imposed by authority with ruthless effectiveness. Angelo is
a disaster. It is questionable whether the public of Vienna
learn from the lesson, but dramatically the point is made
for the audience. Likewise, in *Our Country's Good*, the
Governor argues his case, puts it to the test, and we see
and experience the wisdom of his purpose.

Other officers in the new penal colony show an intelligent
and scientific interest in their surroundings. Johnston
studies the plants, Dawes is mapping the stars, and Collins
is studying the customs of the Indians. Governor Phillip,
however, experiments with social theory and his argument,
as can be seen in the letters that preface this edition of the
play, is the justified premise on which the play is built.

The ending of the play is not a sentimental justification
of theatre as a symbol of liberal education. In social terms
'theatre becomes a means of liberating people, because it
offers them the chance to envision a future in which they
are free, and of creating a community of players which
serves as a paradigm for this utopian society' (Ann Wilson).
In colonial terms the utopian society seems not to include
the native Aborigine, who, like the native in Prospero's
island, might claim 'this island's mine'.

The Aborigine
The Aborigine speaks four times in the play and adds a
further dimension to the action. He represents the native
Australian population who passively observed and later
suffered from the arrival of the British colonists. His
language, albeit English 'of another sort', corresponds to
his native experience and his culture. Essentially he is only
able to perceive the pale-faced newcomers as ghostly
ancestors who have returned to the land. By the end of the
play his physical affliction forces him to a different
conclusion. The Aborigine is no mere token figure. He is
part of the event and offers another interpretation of what
the arrival of the First Fleet signified. In production the
importance of the character has been seen to vary in
relation to how he has been staged.

Robert Hughes distinguished the Australian Aborigines
from the Tahitians and the Maoris in so far as they were
not a settled agricultural people –

> They carried their conception of the sacred, of mythic
> time and ancestral origins with them as they walked.
> These were embodied in the landscape; every hill and
> valley, each kind of animal and tree, had its place in a
> systematic but unwritten whole. Take away this territory
> and they were deprived, not of 'property' but of their
> embodied history, their locus of myth, their 'dreaming'.
> (*The Fatal Shore*, p. 17)

Keith Willey relates how the Dreamtime was to become
nightmare for the Aborigine and expands on the mythic
structure of Aboriginal culture:

> In the Dreamtime the hero ancestors had created all the
> features of the earth. When the task was complete they
> themselves often became rocks and hills and
> watercourses, so that the contours of the land were the
> proof of the old men's teachings. The world was the
> people's own country and that of other tribes, much like
> themselves, extending away into the unknown. The sky
> was a canopy covering all and coming down beyond the

horizon to meet and enclose the flat surface on which men and women followed the fixed patterns of their lives. (*When The Sky Fell Down*, p. 51)

In the last scene of the play it appears as if the Aborigine has become infected – 'Look: oozing pustules on my skin, heat on my forehead.' This could be a physical smallpox contracted from the new settlers, but it is possible that the damage was as much psychological because the fences erected by the colonists broke the Aborigines' songlines, their ancestral pathways. However interpreted, the arrival of the convict fleet was bad news for the native population.

The more strongly the presence of the Aborigine is felt in production the more the play can be seen to be concerned with colonisation. An Australian production, by the Melbourne Theatre Company in 1989, cast an Aboriginal actor (Tom E. Lewis) in the part and this tended to make the issue of native displacement a core feature of the play. He was omnipresent and linked the scenes with music played on the didgeridoo. As one reviewer described him:

> Tom Lewis becomes a positive force – still a spectator and victim, but one who makes haunting comment between scenes with his didgeridoo, giving a hooting, growling dimension . . . (Barry Oakley, *Independent Monthly*, July 1989)

Two love stories

The convict characters are sharply distinguished in the play; they all have past histories which we learn in the course of the action. Sideway, Freeman and Liz Morden each evoke their life in England and their stories are continued during the play. Two, however, Mary Brenham and Duckling Smith, become involved in romantic relationships – with Ralph Clark and Harry Brewer – and these stories form a central thread to the structure of *Our Country's Good*.

The removed penal setting allows the play to focus on how social forces involving class and status can have a psychological effect on sexual relationships. The social

realities are made intensely personal as the two love stories
are acted out before us:

Dabby   When dealing with men, always have a contract.
Mary   Love is a contract.
Dabby   Love is the barter of perishable goods. A man's
word for a woman's body.
Wisehammer   Dabby is right. If a man loves a woman,
he should marry her.
Ralph   Sometimes he can't.
Wisehammer   Then she should look for someone who
can.
Dabby   A woman should look after her own interests,
that's all.
Mary   Her interest is to love. (p. 70)

The experience of transportation and the convicts' play
affects the two pairs in contrasting ways. Ralph undergoes a
sexual liberation, whereas Harry is destroyed. Mary is
transformed ('I love this'), but Duckling ends up
distraught.

Harry Brewer is a study of sexual paranoia. Infatuated,
and in thrall to the younger Duckling, and certain that she
has been unfaithful to him, his jealousy combines with guilt
(for hanging his rival, Handy Baker) to produce the stroke
which kills him. Duckling's situation is invidious. What
little life she has craves freedom and space, but Harry
won't give it to her. Their social identities, as convict and
gaoler, enforce mutual suspicion. The inherent brutality of
her environment and her past experience cause Duckling to
fear the consequences of committing herself to Harry – 'I
loved him . . . I thought that if he knew he would become
cruel'.

Like Harry, Ralph is sexually disturbed at the beginning
of the play. Mortified by the rampant sexual activity he has
witnessed on the voyage from England, he has gained a
reputation for being homosexual because he will have
nothing to do with the women convicts. Now, in Australia,
he is still obsessed with the 'scene of whoredom . . . going
on there in the women's camp'. In response, he practises a

private, introverted sexual ritual which involves the
elevation of his wife to the status of icon, of woman pure
and undefiled.

Between Scene Four, when we first see Ralph alone at
night, and Scene Nine, when he is awaiting midnight in
order to kiss his wife's picture, he has met Mary Brenham
and become even more disturbed. He is drawn to Mary and
now suffers guilt ('Dreamt my beloved Betsey that I was
with you and that I was going to be arrested'). His sexual
frustration is reflected in his thought process as he paces
alone in his tent. His mind jumps from one erotic image to
another – from his 'darling tender wife', to whoredom in
the women's camp, to the harlot who 'kissed with an
impudent face' (in Proverbs), to the flogging of a woman
convict. Both Dabby Bryant and Wisehammer – a rival for
Mary's affection – are well aware of Ralph's interest in
Mary, and distrust him. Under the influence of the play,
however, as they are brought together in rehearsal in the
role of lovers, Mary gradually releases Ralph from the
repression that is revealed as long-standing:

> **Ralph**· I've never looked at the body of a woman
> before.
> **Mary** Your wife?
> **Ralph** It wasn't right to look at her. (p. 79)

Their play provides the environment whereby class and
status cease to inhibit a natural and loving relationship.

A play about theatre

> Rarely has the redemptive, transcendental power of
> theatre been argued with such eloquence and passion.
> (Georgina Brown, *Independent*)

> A moving and affirmative tribute to the transforming
> power of drama itself. (Michael Billington, *Guardian*)

There can be no doubt that the popularity of *Our Country's
Good* with both actors and the public has largely depended
on its powerful affirmation of theatre as a social activity.

The play debates arguments for and against theatre and embraces all the historical prejudices that have been levelled against it, while demonstrating in performance how drama affects people for the good. As Irving Wardle states, 'the play develops into a parable on the civilising force of drama: which it is well able to achieve as the process is acted out rather than described' (*The Times*).

Arguments for and against theatre

For as long as theatre has existed in Western society it has suffered assault and restrictions of one kind or another. Philosophers, religious puritans and governments have all argued or acted against it. These arguments have not concerned what 'kind' of theatre a society ought to have (which has preoccupied critical theorists) but have been aimed at the very nature of 'acting' and of 'plays'. Major Ross carries many of these, often irrational, opinions in *Our Country's Good*.

An early philosophical objection to theatre and acting is found in Plato's *Republic* which does not so much criticise the Athenian theatre of his day as the 'Idea' of a theatre. According to Plato

> Everything that exists, or happens, in this world is an imperfect copy of an ideal object or action or state that has an ideal existence beyond this world. The productions of the poets (and artists) are therefore imitations of imperfect copies of an ideal life; they are third-hand and unreal, and can teach us nothing of value about life. (T. S. Dorsch, *Classical Literary Criticism*, 1965)

On a more practical level, Plato also argued that the act of impersonation was dangerous for the actor because imitation is formative. To act a bad or immoral character would directly corrupt the actor. As for the audience, they were endangered by having their perception distorted through emotional involvement with the action. These were more developed arguments than that of Solon who accused

Thespis, who gave his name to the art of acting, of being a
liar because he pretended to be someone else.

In England, throughout the Middle Ages, drama was
controlled by the Church. The Mystery cycles and Morality
plays were, essentially, propaganda for institutionalised
Christianity. Then when theatre began to take on secular
and professional aspects in the sixteenth century both the
government and the Puritans recognised a threat – to
political and religious orthodoxy. Official censorship of
plays passed from the Master of the Revels to the Lord
Chamberlain's office, and their powers were further
formalised in the Stage Licensing Act of 1737. The
government's power to censor any public performance
lasted until as late as 1968. Censorship was intended to
protect the Church, royality, government and public
decency from the danger of free speech emanating from the
public stage.

What particularly obsessed the puritan faction in
sixteenth- and seventeenth-century England, apart from an
innate horror of pleasure and recreation, was the idea that
the theatre displayed sexual relations and sexual activity
and that this was bound to corrupt those who witnessed
plays. The young were especially in peril. There was,
furthermore, the very real possibility that theatre could
mock those in authority. The Puritans had a brief triumph
in 1642 when the theatres were closed down during
Cromwell's administration. At the Restoration in 1660,
Charles II permitted actresses to perform for the first time
on the English stage and this allowed for another, long-
lasting, prejudice to develop – that 'actresses are not famed
for their morals'.

Jonas Barish, in *The Antitheatrical Prejudice* (1981),
points out that:

> One recurrent feature of the history of the theatre is the
> fact that outbursts of antitheatrical sentiment tend to
> coincide with the flourishing of the theatre itself. The
> stage provokes the most active and sustained hostility
> when it becomes a vital force in the life of the

community. It is then that its own values seem most dangerously to collide with the received values of church and state. (p. 66)

The survival of live theatre, even through this century in the face of radio, film, television and video, is perhaps the strongest argument in its favour. That it should occasionally 'flourish', become 'a vital force' and have 'its own values' demands recognition. The essentially social significance of theatre and acting was recognised by Hamlet who defines its purpose –

> to hold as 'twere the mirror up to nature; to show virtue her feature, scorn her own image, and the very age and body of the time his form and pressure. (III.ii.21–24)

He warns Polonius (noted apologist for the received values of the state) that the actors are 'the abstract and brief chronicles of the time. After your death you were better have a bad epitaph than their ill report while you live' (II.ii.520–22).

Hamlet's image of the theatre as the mirror which reflects the times assumes the communicative aspect of talking and listening which is basic to theatre as it is to living. As Terence Hawkes explains:

> of all the forms of art in which societies engage, drama remains the only one which wholly derives from and fully exploits the central fact of man's 'talking' nature. In general terms, drama celebrates, manifests, and is 'about' the complex reality of man as the 'talking animal'. In particular, it draws upon the full range of verbal and non-verbal activities involved in 'talking'. If language is man's distinctive feature, drama is his distinctive art. (*Shakespeare's Talking Animals*, 1973)

Theatre in Crisis: the immediate context

From one perspective the British theatre can be seen to have flourished during the last thirty years. The Royal Court Theatre in London has produced an impressive range of new dramatists. The Royal Shakespeare Company and the Royal National Theatre have gained world-wide reputations for their classic and modern repertoires. New theatre buildings and companies have become established throughout Britain. Over one hundred and fifty plays can be seen in London venues, large and small, at any time. However, in 1988 a large gathering of the theatre profession and academics met at the University of London to consider a 'Theatre in Crisis'. What was the problem?

The Theatre in Crisis conference fully recognised how dependent the British theatre was on government subsidy, and this was being cut back. Theatrical activity is either commercial (ruled by the profit motive and symbolised by the 'West End' musical), amateur, or subsidised – that is, helped by outside funding, hitherto mostly by the government agency the Arts Council. Unquestionably, the high standard of British theatre in recent years has been achieved with the help of subsidy. Government policy was now encouraging the arts to gain their sponsorship from 'the private sector' – which would almost certainly determine what was allowed to be produced. In brief, the conference argued that 'a free market economy and private sponsorship cannot guarantee the necessary conditions for theatre to fulfil its many functions.'

Timberlake Wertenbaker's *Our Country's Good* was a timely reminder of what theatre is for, as Stafford-Clark recognised:

> Not the least of the play's achievements was the resonant chord it touched in London's beleaguered theatrical community. A play that proclaimed the power and enduring worth of theatre, and that celebrated its centrality to our lives, was of importance in the third term of a government who deemed subsidy a dirty word.

Theatre in action
Our Country's Good ends on a positive and triumphant note with the assured success of the convicts' production of

The Recruiting Officer. Such a success is the more
powerfully affecting because, for most of the play, it
appears so improbable.

The convicts are all brutalised and desperate to begin
with, and none has any experience of acting. They have
varied motives for joining the cast, mainly to do with self-
interest. There is a hostility between the women emanating
from dislike of Liz Morden. As soon as rehearsing begins
four of the cast are under threat of severe punishment,
possibly hanging. Ralph Clark takes responsibility for the
production at first merely to be noticed by the Governor.
Then his worthy attempt to direct is frustrated by the
inexperience of the cast. The other officers do not help with
the production and Major Ross does his best to destroy it.
Despite all this, however, the play takes a hold on all those
involved with it, to the extent that it gradually becomes
their main purpose for living.

The scenes of incompetent rehearsal, which are very
funny, are set against an ongoing dialectic which concerns
the meaning and significance of theatre. So theory is put to
an active test. Essentially the Governor believes that 'the
theatre is an expression of civilisation' and his support of
the convicts' play derives from motives that are both
realistic and idealistic:

> Some of these men will have finished their sentence in a
> few years. They will become members of society again,
> and help create a new society in this colony. Should we
> not encourage them now to think in a free and
> responsible manner? (p. 21)

It becomes vital, therefore, that the experience of theatre is
seen to have a beneficial influence on the convict cast – for
their own sakes and the sake of the colony. By extension,
the play makes its own case for the value of liberal
education, in particular theatre, in the lives of the socially
deprived.

The traditional arguments offered for and against the
convicts being allowed to perform are made 'dramatic'
because they emerge from the personalities of the officer

characters. Ralph has doubts but learns from experience
that the convicts, while rehearsing, 'seemed to acquire a
dignity'; Collins is judicious and fair; Tench is
unimaginative; the Reverend Johnson is obsessed with
moral propriety. However the full weight of opposition and
anti-theatrical prejudice ('reasons he has not made quite
clear') is carried by Major Robbie Ross. He hates the
convicts and the idea of the play with equal vehemence. In
mitigation it could be argued that Ross is a trained
professional military officer, not a prison guard, that he is
bound to question anything that might 'teach
insubordination, disobedience, revolution' (i.e. the play),
and that he hates the 'hellish hole' which is Australia.

However Ross's treatment of the convicts borders on the
sadistic and it is in the face of his fury that the power of the
play's influence on the convicts is most thrillingly
demonstrated. In Act Two Scene Five, while Ross is
humiliating Sideway, Dabby and Mary Brenham in front of
the cast

> *Sideway turns to Liz and starts acting, boldly, across the*
> *room, across everyone.*

and Farquhar's lines take on a new significance in this
immediate context:

> **Sideway**   What pleasures I may receive abroad are
> indeed uncertain; but this I am sure of, I shall meet with
> less cruelty among the most barbarous nations than I
> have found at home.

The acting of Sideway and Liz is both dignified and defiant
and has an heroic dimension. It is most effective in
performance because it is so unexpected.

Similarly, Act Two Scene Ten ends with a surprising and
uplifting speech from Liz which shows how she has
developed under the influence of the play. Beginning as
'one of the most difficult women in the colony . . . Lower
than a slave, full of loathing, foul mouthed, desperate' she
is now encouraged to perform well by the Governor. She
replies

> Your Excellency, I will endeavour to speak Mr
> Farquhar's lines with the elegance and clarity their own
> worth commands.

The simple eloquence of the sentence, coming from Liz,
has a stunning effect in the theatre.

Act One of *Our Country's Good* is concerned with the
setting-up of the convict play to the point of the first
rehearsal (which ends in a shambles). Act Two increasingly
shows how the cast are affected by their commitment to
their roles. Dabby Bryant's refusal to be impressed by the
play she is in helps maintain a sense of balance. There is no
exaggerated sentiment attached to the business of theatre.
What emerges as the most 'civilising' influence of the
experience is the gradual development of mutual
recognition and sympathy among the convict cast. Through
their commitment to the production they become
committed to each other and 'despised prisoners' no longer.

The sound of applause and laughter with which the play
ends involves the two audiences in the social ritual of
theatre. The audience watching *Our Country's Good* are
made emphatically aware of their 'role' in the theatrical
event. To an extent their very presence is given communal
approval and justification by the triumph of the convicts'
play. Theatre itself has been shown to be worthwhile. This
aspect of *Our Country's Good*, whereby it continuously
draws attention to itself as a play, places it as a classic of
the kind known as 'metatheatre' or 'metadrama'.

Theatrical self-referral takes many forms. Shakespeare's
Love's Labour's Lost and *A Midsummer Night's Dream*
end with a play within the play, performed by spectacularly
bad 'actors'. Both are great fun, both contribute to the
general themes of the larger play, and both allow
Shakespeare to offer a subtle advertisement for his own
'professional' company of actors. *Hamlet* also contains a
'play within the play' but goes further in making the Players
and 'playing' central to the concerns of the main play.
Hamlet himself talks with authority on the nature of theatre
and acting, and stage-manages *The Mousetrap*. The play

also contains theatrical in-jokes which would have pleased
the contemporary audience – such as when Polonius tells
Hamlet that 'I did enact Julius Caesar. I was killed i' th'
Capitol; Brutus killed me'. He is talking to the actor
(Richard Burbage) who would actually have played Brutus
and who is going to kill him again in this play. Pirandello's
Six Characters in Search of an Author uses the theatre as a
metaphor to philosophise on life. In *Waiting for Godot*
Beckett has Vladimir and Estragon enact theatrical
'routines' and when Vladimir finally says 'At me too
someone is looking, of me too someone is saying, he is
sleeping, he knows nothing, let him sleep on' he is referring
to the audience who are observing him in the theatre.
Other plays have dealt with 'backstage' life, exploiting the
egotism of actors for comic effect – Harwood's *The Dresser*
and Frayn's *Noises Off* are examples.

Our Country's Good is full of theatrical reference. The
original production with its blatant doubling of characters,
was consciously 'theatrical'. The on-going debate
concerning the value of theatre would inevitably have a
heightened significance for an audience watching the play.
And the rehearsals, which involve much discussion on the
nature of theatrical convention and the role of actor and
audience, as well as demonstrating good and bad
performance, are steeped in theatrical lore which any
audience will enjoy.

Language and identity

Where did the wee Lieutenant learn to speak? (Act One
Scene Six)

Speak in English, Wisehammer. (Act Two Scene One)

When Governor Phillip argues that by speaking Farquhar's
language 'the convicts will be speaking a refined, literate
language and expressing sentiments of a delicacy they are
not used to' his intention is not to impose a superior
language upon them. He continues – 'It will remind them

that there is more to life than crime, punishment.' Again, when Ralph Clark claims of the convicts that 'saying those well-balanced lines of Mr Farquhar, they seemed to acquire a dignity, they seemed – they seemed to lose some of their corruption', it is the human potential of the convicts that is underlined rather than Farquhar's language. Arscott proves the Governor right, in his case: 'I don't have to remember the things I've done, when I speak Kite's lines I don't hate any more.' The experience of their involvement with *The Recruiting Officer* is liberating for all the convicts, not because they have assumed a higher culture, but because they have regained a sense of their own identities. These identities, largely quashed at the beginning of the play, are always recognisable by the way they speak. All the characters in *Our Country's Good* have their own way of speaking and their different voices are an essential element in the play's recognition of how society is made up of individuals rather than groups.

From the beginning we see how the convicts are regarded and treated by their custodians. Subjugation and hideous brutality are the norm, to the extent that the prisoners are reduced symbolically and actually to silence – 'Fear whispers, screams, falls silent, hushed'. Mary Brenham, when she first tries to speak, does so 'inaudibly'. Their humanity is suppressed. When Arscott is given 200 lashes for trying to escape we hear 'It will take time for him to see himself as a human being again.' As with prisoners throughout history the convicts are depersonalised in the eyes of their gaolers and demeaned through generalisation. Wisehammer describes the convicts as 'alone, frightened, nameless'.

Prisoners are still given a uniform and a number today (see the letter headings which preface this book). In the play the transported prisoners are variously described as a 'bunch of convicts', 'sinners', 'the bone idle', 'filthy, thieving, lying whores' and 'vice-ridden vermin' for good measure. Such pejorative classification of individuals is the pernicious habit of the self-righteous, even fascist, element in society, ever keen to find a scapegoat in order to assert themselves against whoever might form an 'underclass', be it 'the Jews' or 'the Blacks' or 'the Irish'.

In *Our Country's Good* Wisehammer is Jewish, Caesar is Black and James Freeman is Irish. Dabby Bryant comes from Devon, Sideway and Liz Morden are from London. In performance these characters have a 'voice' that distinguishes them as individuals and unique personalities, despite their being brought together by the immediate circumstance of transportation. At some point in the play all the convicts speak for themselves, and differently. James (Ketch) Freeman, for example, has an emotive Irish earnestness and occasional lyricism (Act One Scene Nine) whereas Robert Sideway is given to vivid histrionic description (Act One Scene Five). Sideway is also capable, when angry, of slipping into a 'canting' tongue which is the peculiar argot of Liz Morden when she tells her life story at the start of Act Two.

Robert Hughes in *The Fatal Shore* writes about 'canting' talk:

> The otherness of the convict was further reinforced by his language, for his argot declared that he came from another society, an Alsatia of the mind. The linguistic class barriers in penal Australia were absolute – the very opposite of today, when all classes share the robust vernacular of Australian slang. English criminal cant, an entire sub-language, immediately branded its users and the aspiring Emancipist had to unlearn it or stay where he was. (p. 345)

The progression of Liz is a key story in *Our Country's Good*. She is chosen by Governor Phillip to be in the play 'to be made an example of . . . by redemption . . . of her humanity'. She develops under the influence of working together with the other convict actors to a point where she has to 'speak'

Collins For the good of the colony.
Phillip And of the play. (p. 82)

From being 'lower than a slave, full of loathing, foul
mouthed' she is brought to a point where she makes a
moral decision that will have a profound effect on
everybody. She grows to realise that she has an identity
that is significant. Hitherto her identity – her voice – has
been worthless:

> **Phillip** Why wouldn't you say any of this before?
> **Liz** Because it wouldn't have mattered.
> **Phillip** Speaking the truth?
> **Liz** Speaking. (p. 82)

The officers' manner of speech also helps to define their
dramatic significance. Governor Phillip and Captain Collins
(Advocate General) are educated, civilised and cultured.
Their clear and judicious arguments command respect.
Major Ross and Captain Campbell, linked by their
common Scottishness (Keneally mentions 'Caledonian
bile'), have different speech patterns. Ross is so fixed in his
puritanical sense of values that he is quite incapable of
considering any leniency towards the convicts. His
irrational position is reflected in a personalised form of
rhetorical abuse invented by Timberlake Wertenbaker. He
simply cannot find the words to articulate his anger and
disgust so the writer gives him an original invective which
conveys how suspect his position is. His acolyte, Campbell,
is equally out of place as a convict overseer and his
language reflects this. The telegramatic brevity of his
expression, broken up with expletives of pure sound,
suggests an inability to think beyond a very limited range of
military experience. He does, however, in a completely
unsubtle way, indicate his honest appreciation of the
Farquhar play – so adding further weight against the
intransigence of Robbie Ross.

Staging the play

The dramatic structure of *Our Country's Good* makes
particular demands on all practitioners – director, actors,

designer and stage-management. The twenty-two scenes of
the play alternate between sizeable groups of convicts or
marine officers and more intimate scenes involving only two
people, with the lone Aborigine posing a further staging
challenge. The scenes also alternate between day and night,
with consequent shifts in mood. The audience is invited to
engage with the ideas of the play and with the emotional
weight of involvement with characters and relationships. As
ever, the director's responsibility is to 'find' the rhythm
inherent in the play so that the cumulative building of
emotion is sustained. Speaking as an actor, Ron Cook
explains what is involved:

> I think of the play as a series of emotional tube stations.
> You can do one scene, and then be off for a while, and
> then there are the major intersections when everyone is
> on together. What surprised me was the audience
> response at the end. We weren't aware of the whole
> emotional journey for the audience – what an emotional
> roller-coaster the audience goes on.

Scene changes need to be as speedy as possible. For the
emotional development to be effective each scene has then
to be played with full regard for the reality of the situation,
which is predominantly dark. There is wit and comedy in
the play, mostly connected with the problems of convicts
rehearsing, but the comedy emerges only if the characters
are in earnest. They are convicts, not actors, and they don't
want to be where they are. *Our Country's Good* is not a
fun play about theatre conventions in the manner of *Noises
Off* (Frayn) or *The Real Inspector Hound* (Stoppard).
Above all, it tells a story which is neither too solemn nor
too funny.

Staging the play concerns, primarily, acting and
scenography and the experience of the 1988 Royal Court
Theatre production may be used to reflect on both these
aspects. The very fact that the play was commissioned by
the Royal Court provides a clue. At the Royal Court for
many years the most significant figure has been the
playwright. The theatre prides itself on being Britain's

National Theatre of 'new writing' and has championed most of the dramatists who have emerged significantly since 1956. Consequently the word takes precedence and scenography is a strict servant to the word. *Our Country's Good* is consciously 'theatrical', regularly drawing attention to itself as a play, and as such certain scenographic questions are posed. For example, the original cast consisted of ten actors, four of them women and two of them (one man and one woman) black. The play was actually written with 'doubling' of parts in mind, and in Scene Six, where the Authorities Discuss the Merits of the Theatre, the four women played men. There was no attempt to create a wholly naturalistic world. When actors adopted a different costume for a different part this was done, frequently, on stage, in sight of the audience. An actress playing a convict, simply by putting on a military jacket, became a marine officer.

What is then created is a 'stage reality', perfectly acceptable to an audience, who would, from the start, have realised that no attempt was being made to offer a window onto the world of eighteenth-century Australia. Of course the stage reality does involve 'Australia', where the action is set, and where the scenes are either outdoors in daylight or set at night. Lighting then becomes the most effective means technically of suggesting Australia. The harsh blue and the immensity of the sky might be indicated by lighting a cyclorama upstage (or the walls of a more intimate studio space). Sound can be used to suggest setting and space by the sensitive introduction of the sea – breaking on the ship before Scene One, and fed in subsequently during the play.

Costume defines the status of the characters and the play requires only minimal changes of costume. Likewise the play requires relatively few props on stage. Mostly the scenes require only one or two props and five scenes require none at all (for example – Scene One requires flogging equipment; Scene Three, guns – or one gun; Scene Four, table, journal, pen and ink; Scene Five, copy of the play and handkerchief, and so on). It becomes very

important, however, that these props be historically
correct. Beyond this, the stage reality depends upon the
acting.

 Our Country's Good is fraught with difficulties for the
actor eager to win affection. Many of the characters are
unattractive, either in appearance or in attitude – inevitably
so, given their situation. Despite this, however, the many
productions that have followed that of the Royal Court,
both in Britain and abroad, provide ample evidence of how
rewarding the play is to prepare and perform. Each one of
the twenty-two characters has an 'inner' life and an
individual 'voice', as we have seen, and these must be
found by the actor. Apart from the technical skill required
to play more than one character – if doubling is used –
there is also the need to be able to show the progression of
characters through the play whenever they appear in a new
scene.

 The technical demands may be illustrated by one,
admittedly extreme, example taken from Act Two Scene
Nine – 'A Love Scene'. Here Mary Brenham is rehearsing
alone at night. At the end of Scene Seven she has left the
stage in great distress because of the imminent hanging of
Liz. Only the one speech of Duckling (Scene Eight)
intervenes before Mary is back on stage to practise her role
as Sylvia. She is now in control. Immediately the actress
has to convey how far Mary has developed in confidence
from earlier in the play, though she remains – however
hard she tries – an amateur when it comes to acting. But
there are more things to consider. What Mary is rehearsing
is a part of *The Recruiting Officer* where Sylvia herself is
'acting' the role of Jack Wilful, who is a man:

> *She tries that again, with a stronger and lower voice.*
> *Ralph comes on, sees her. She sees him, but continues.*
> (p. 77)

How is she to continue? Alone, at night, with the man who
has been showing ever-increasing interest in her? It is likely
that the delivery of her lines as Sylvia/Jack Wilful will be
newly affected by his presence. The actress of Mary has to

convey all these shifts to an audience. Furthermore the actress has to convey the irony and the poignancy of what Mary is saying, while it is probable that Mary herself does not see it. However, an astute audience should pick up on the significance of what Mary is saying to Ralph, in Farquhar's words, in this particular context:

> 'put on the man of honour, and tell me plainly what usage I must expect when I'm under your command . . . and now you are my Captain.' (p. 77–8)

Further reading

Background material for *Our Country's Good*

Clark, Ralph, *The Journals and Letters of Lieutenant Ralph Clark* (ed. Paul G. Fidlon; Australian Documents Library, 1981)

Endelman, Todd M., *The Jews in Georgian England 1714–1830* (The Jewish Publication Society of America, 1979)

Farquhar, George, *The Recruiting Officer* (New Mermaid Edition, ed. J. Ross; London, 1991)

Hawkins, David T., *Bound for Australia* (Phillimore & Co, 1987)

Hughes, Robert, *The Fatal Shore* (Collins, 1987)

Keneally, Thomas, *Outback* (Coronet, 1984)

Keneally, Thomas, *The Playmaker* (Sceptre, 1988)

Mayhew, Henry, *London's Underworld* (ed. Peter Quennell; Bracken Books, 1983)

Rosenthal, R., and Jacobsen, L., *Pygmalion in the Classroom* (Holt, Rinehart and Winston, 1968)

Stafford-Clark, Max, *Letters to George* (Nick Hern Books, 1989)

Tench, Watkin, *A Narrative of the Expedition to Botany Bay* (London, 1789)

Willey, Keith, *When the Sky Fell Down: The Destruction of the Tribes of the Sydney Region 1788–1850s* (Collins, 1979)

Dictionaries of criminal slang and cant: Grose, Francis, *A Classical Dictionary of the Vulgar Tongue* (London, 1785); and Partridge, Eric, *A Dictionary of the Underworld*, (3rd ed., London, 1971)

On Timberlake Wertenbaker and *Our Country's Good*

The most comprehensive bibliography on Timberlake Wertenbaker and *Our Country's Good* can be found in *New Theatre Quarterly*, Vol. IX, No. 35, August 1993, compiled by Susan Carlson, who writes about the different critical reactions to productions of the play in London, Australia and the United States of America, in 'Issues of Identity, Nationality, and Performance: the Reception of Two Plays by Timberlake Wertenbaker'.

Reviews of the Royal Court's production are collected in the *London Theatre Record* for 9–22 September 1988 and 30 July–12 August 1989.

Articles

Borg, Dominica, 'New Wave on a Fatal Shore: Timberlake Wertenbaker's *Our Country's Good*' in *Theater Three*, 9, 1990

Rabey, David Ian, 'Defining Difference: Timberlake Wertenbaker's Drama of Language, Dispossession and Discovery' in *Modern Drama*, 33, 1990

Wilson, Ann, '*Our Country's Good*: Theatre, Colony and Nation in Wertenbaker's Adaptation of *The Playmaker*' in *Modern Drama*, 34, 1991

Preface

In the summer of 1988, I went to HMP Wormwood Scrubs with the actors of *Our Country's Good*, the director Max Stafford-Clark and Philip Howard, the assistant director. We went to see a performance of Howard Barker's *The Love of a Good Man*, performed by long-term prisoners, that is, prisoners convicted of the most serious crimes. It was an unforgettable evening. We huddled in the forecourt as the prison gates closed behind us, and then were led through the courtyard: high walls, barbed wire – upstairs to the barking of guard dogs and finally into a small room. But, once the play began, we were at the theatre: the intensity of the performances, the extremely good acting of some of the prisoners, the understanding they seemed to have of this complex play, made it a riveting evening. Afterwards, they were as happy and eager for praise as any actors after a good performance, but we only had five minutes before we watched them being led back to their cells.

That night was pivotal for the acting and writing of *Our Country's Good*: it confirmed all our feelings about the power and the value of theatre.

Some months later I received the first letter from Joe White. Other letters followed, from other prisoners. (I have printed these in full, unedited.) Joe White then asked me if he could put on *Our Country's Good* at Blundeston prison, Lowestoft, where he had been transferred. Philip Howard and I went to see it. It seemed to me the play had come full circle, performed in that prison room with an intensity and accuracy playwrights dream of and I remember relishing the wit with which the prisoners portrayed the officers of the play.

As I write this, many Education Departments of prisons are being cut – theatre comes under the Education Department – and the idea of tough punishment as justice seems to be gaining ground in our increasingly harsh society. I hope these letters speak for themselves and, indeed, for our world.

Timberlake Wertenbaker
London, June 1991

Letters from Joe White

N55463 J. White
D Wing
H.M.P. Blundeston
Lowestoft
SUFFOLK,
NR32 5BG
April 1989

Dear Timberlake,

It seems an age since the production of 'The Love Of A Good Man' at the 'Scrubs'. Within a couple of months the 'inside' cast was split up and moved to various far flung parts of the country.

Firstly a belated congratulations on your award for 'Our Country's Good'. I did manage to have a read of the script, Eve White – one of the actresses – brought a copy in for us to read. Of course I'd much rather have been able to see a performance, but, there you go. Reading through the play, there were moments of ghostly familiarity, uncanny likenesses.

Secondly, the compliments you gave to our play in the various reviews of 'Our Country's Good', did not pass unnoticed. Not to mention the 'plug' you gave us all on actually receiving your award. It is difficult for me to explain the sense of achievement and feelings of pride it gave not only myself and the rest of the cast, but also to our families and friends. It spoke volumes. Thank you.

Mac, who played the Prince of Wales in 'The Love Of . . .' was moved to a prison on the Isle of Shepey, where he is making moves to start a drama group. Here at Blundeston, I was lucky enough to meet up with a fellow 'lifer' that I'd previously acted with in another Scrubs production, Steven Berkoff's 'East'. Lee subsequently wrote a play 'Timecycles' about prison life, based around some of Steve's material. We set to work getting it put on here. I had a bash at directing, and I'm happy to say the first (of many hopefully) Blundeston plays was performed last month to the rest of the guys in here. It was quite an experience for all concerned. You wouldn't believe the amount of energy and patience needed to get it all together. Maybe you would – a universal aspect of the theatre?

Basically the spirit lives on. Prison is about failure normally, and how we are reminded of it each day of every year. Drama, and self-expression in general, is a refuge and one of the only real weapons against the hopelessness of these places. I believe you gained the insight to recognise this, it is evident in your writing.

Theatre is, of course, an essential part of all society, and I'm glad to say that it is alive and kicking within these walls. Long may it do so. Again many, many thanks, and I look forward to reading more of your work.

Yours sincerely,

Joe White

(Hacker)

Dear Timberlake,
                    Thank you for your letter, I had meant to
reply sooner but its been a particularly hectic few weeks for me,
both emotionally and physically.

Firstly, I'm sorry that I was unable to speak to you on the
phone, in person, the other week. I'm afraid its one of those
infuriating procedures that it does no-one any good trying to
fathom out. I thought it worth a try though, to see if (by some
miracle) you could have got away at such short notice. Perhaps
in the future, if you were interested and given a little more pre-
warning, you could come to our next production?

"TIMECYCLES" has finally come to a close. We've just
finished editing a video of the invited audience performance. Its
proved not only an interesting experience but has also served as
a great tonic against the Post-Production Blues.

"TIMECYCLES" was a play that attempted to face the
realities of prison life, by focusing on the effects of prison on
individuals – rather than on the political quagmire that
surrounds these institutions. During the brief opportunity I had
to talk to the audience afterwards, it soon became apparent that
they were more concerned with the actual event itself and the
constituent parts of the production, rather than the subject
matter. I wonder if you have experienced anything similar, with
view to your own work? Maybe it was a case of the audience's
attention to the play, merging with their impressions of entering
a prison, and that the real impact of the play would register
once outside again?

It obviously means a great deal to receive praise for a
performance as an actor, but I can't help feeling this should be
secondary to the reaction the play has, or has failed, to provoke
in the audience. I felt like pointing out that most of what they
had seen portrayed in drama, was actually happening, at that
very moment, not a hundred yards away. In this respect I still
feel that the play failed, in that this connection was not seen to
be made. Am I expecting too much do you think? Could it be
that a plays impact on an audience is more subtle? I'm sure,
having directed the play and its subject being so poignant for
me, has had a lot to do with this stress on the importance of

meaning. I feel it is an instructive lesson though, as long as it doesn't lead to excessive depression!

As for the future, I have been in contact with Snoo Wilson and would dearly love to produce "The Glad Hand" here, hopefully early in the new year. I believe it was first produced at the Royal Court and directed by Max in 78. It really is such a challenging play and so different from "TIMECYCLES". It would allow full reign to both the actors and the stage crew's imagination, as opposed to the excessive amounts of personal experience needed for "TIMECYCLES". Snoo has expressed a wish to attend rehearsals, and what with the chances of a director being employed here still being slim, I would be doubly keen to have him present, if only sporadically. I am very excited about this new project.

Charles Vance came to see "TIMECYCLES" and has promised us a piece in the Amateur Stage. He also offered his services to take a couple of 'master acting classes' – I wish I knew what they were! I must admit to being a little dubious about this, as I'm not entirely sure we're on the same wavelength. I suppose it would be a good experience either way though?

I'm really pleased that "Our Country's Good" is back at the Court. Some of my family are hoping to get to see it. I did write to Max ages ago, giving him my whole-hearted permission to reprint my letter to you in the programme, if he so wished. I fear, though, that it is possible my letter failed to reach him, prison mail being almost as undependable as the telephone system is unreachable!

Anyway, I trust all is going well and I look forward to reading the new script. If you do wish to send Stanislavsky's book it would be gratefully received. There is no problem, thank goodness, abouts books being sent into prison. They are a lifeline to me. I hope to hear from you soon.

Best wishes,

Joe x.

11.3.90

Dear Timberlake,

Thank you for your letter, bearing the good news enabling us to set to work on 'Our Country's Good' I can't believe that was over a month ago. I really have meant to write sooner. It has been such a busy month. Hopefully, Frances will have conveyed to you mine, and the rest of the cast's great pleasure and excitement at the news. I was particularly touched by your own enthusiasm for the production, and I am looking forward immensely to hearing your responses to our work.

Initially, I found it strange to be working on a play that I already held a strong emotional attachment to and involvement with. Combined with the fact that I was working with a director again – therefore having to relinquish the reigns of artistic control, albeit willingly – has lead to feelings of uncertainty as to how much I should contribute to rehearsals. I was very conscious of not wanting to tread on our director's toes. It's possible that I've been cautious about writing to you about the play because of this.

Everything has come together extremely well I feel. There have been wonderful moments of sharing experiences among the cast. Everyone has brought something important to the play. There have also been, seemingly, strange tricks of reality when the play and our situation have overlapped merging the borders of the creative process and actuality.

I am finding the character of Ralph Clark a challenging and an enjoyable role. His naivete is perhaps akin to my own when first entering the prison system. There is also the touch of the romantic about him I feel and maybe in spite of his seriousness, a comic element too. Anyway you shall judge for yourself.

The Royal Court, namely Max Stafford-Clark and Jennifer Cook, have been wonderfully helpful, with press contacts and the loan of costumes. All in all I feel strongly that this production was meant to be.

I look forward to seeing you.

With Best Wishes,

Joe White.

Dear Timberlake,

Of course you have my permission to use any extracts from my letters that you think might be suitable to use in an introduction to 'Our Country's Good'.

I have always been lucky in that I have always discovered close affinities with the various scripts I've worked on. 'Our Country's Good', though, is a play I feel I developed a very special relationship with and I am extremely happy to be involved in this way. Billy, I have spoken to and he is delighted at the prospect – I believe he intends to write to you himself. Perhaps you could send me a copy of the republished edition somewhen, as my present one shows all the signs of a well-worked script!

I shall be moving to Norwich in the early N. Year to an annexed section of Norwich Prison. It is a more open prison, with, I'm informed, 'a very progressive attitude'. We shall soon see. The place certainly sports an impressively heraldic name, Britannia! I'm hopeful of establishing links with the nearby University and possibly the Maddermarket Theatre, where I once worked on a voluntary basis many moons ago.

A production company is showing enormous interest – perhaps too much – in making possibly two programmes for Channel 4, regarding the proposed Crime and Punishment project. Firstly, in the form of an Art documentary, with the idea of following a prison production through various stages of rehearsal and secondly, a full blown television drama of the finished production to run alongside the documentary. Considering Norwich hasn't even a drama group as yet, its still *very* early days – it is all very exciting none-the-less, I hope something comes of it all.

Yes, I would be interested in reading 'The Possessed', I have a great deal of spare time these days.

Best Wishes,

Joe

Letter from Greg Stabler-Smith

G. STABLER-SMITH
N56002 D. WING.
H.M. PRISON
WORMWOOD SCRUBS
DU CANE ROAD
LONDON W12 0AE.

11.2.89

Dear Timberlake,

        Just a few lines to thank you, for mentioning us the drama group, I'm sure that Joe, Mac, Colin and Rick all join me in saying thankyou.

Being able to do the play alone was an unbelievable insight and experience for us all, but the feedback completely blew our minds.

Memories from prison are on the whole negative but having the part of Clout is one positive memory I won't forget.

Eve one of the actress's from 'A good man' first brought in Our Countrys good which we read as a group and really enjoyed, but now we have the same problem. Joe Mac and Colin have moved onto other nicks and I shall be on my way soon.

What you said to the Guardian and on the Olivia awards (Our director videoed it) was really special to us, it will take me a long time to forget and as they say, I've got plenty of time (laughter.)

Must close now thanks and takecare

Greg.

15.2.89.
P.S. I've just been told I'll be moving to Lewes prison in a few weeks so thats put the clamp on another play here for me, but I've heard there's a drama group down there, I'll have to see what the material is like, I don't really want to go back to Ray Cooney after Berkoff & Barker.

Bye.

Letters from Billy Reid

In replying to this letter, please write on the envelope:
Number L15979   Name Reid – Billy M.C.

> B Wing 124
> HM Prison Blundeston
> Lowestoft
> Suffolk NR32 5BG

> 7 June 90

Hullo Timberlake,

Billy Reid here, (I played Harry in O.C's.G.).
I had a read of your letter. Thanx for the compliments, and
Thanx again for making it all possible. I'm sorry I didn't get to
Thank you personally after our performance, not that I feel it
matters now, but I just thot I'd mention it.

It's good to know you were happy with our interpretation of
O.C's.G. It was all a Bran U scene to me, I mean where I come
from in Glasgow there isn't any Drama or Theatre. Wot a pity!
Maybe after my release I could go back and spread the script. I
should've picked up enough exp by then. In Glasgow theres so
much mischanneled energy you wouldn't believe. Youngsters
with real potential who want to be good or the best at
something. Usually, because of the options, they become good at
stealing, chatting up Girls or fighting, or, like me, getting the
jail, HA! HA!

I'm glad I took the plunge into Drama when I did. Initially I
joined to refine my speech and learn how to communicate with
other people. Those reasons must come across really stupid to
someone like yourself who knows a lot about the theatrical
world, well wotever I got a lot-lot more than wot I'd expected.
That wasn't all down to the acting side of it but more down to
O.C's.G. and the part of Harry. I got so much out of that 1
play. I was already on the Road but doing O.C's.G. gave me the
opportunity to take a short cut on my own Road to Reality. I
mean just tying my hair back or getting it cut out of my face
would've taken me yonx to do wot with the scars and blind left
eye. I've since put my hair back to it's natural state,
wild'n'curly, tying it back served a purpose because now if I get

a part that calls for me to have short-looking hair I won't hesitate to tie and gel it back, I aint so weak in that area no more. That was the first time in 9 years the top $\frac{1}{2}$ of my face had seen the light of day.

Thanx again

Billy

Timberlake
PS. I KNOW YOU'RE BUSY OUT THERE SO DON'T BOTHER WORRYING ABOUT WRITING BACK. I JUST WANTED TO SAY THANX.

8 Nov. 90

Hullo Again Timberlake,

Billy Reid here. I hope all is well with you and yours out there. I'm doing allright back here.

I was out on a 4 day home leave, when I came back Joe let me see your letter. Sorry I haven't replied any sooner than now. Anyway Timberlake I'd be honoured to give my permission for you to publish my letter in whole or in part for the republication of O.C's.G.

Since doing O.C's.G. I haven't been into any thing to do with the Drama, that don't mean I'm giving up on it, I quit the Drama because I was going thru a particularly difficult phase and didn't want to draw any heat towards the Drama Group, as it happened anyway, the Group weren't getting any real encouragement because of the internal scene. It's a real pity the people who make the rules can't, or wont, see the sort of benifit a person can get from acting while doing a sentence. I thot after doing O.C's.G. with all its possitive feedback, we'd have gotten a lot more help. We couldn't have asked for any better than the Guardian gave us. Obviously it didn't go down too well with someone with enough weight to block the Drama Groups progress, it's real sad when people like THAT are allowed to make such decisions.

Before I went on home leave I did hear there'd been a discussion about the Drama Group, music group and the prison magazine, which was an idea of mine, I've yet to find out the result of the discussion.

Well that's about it for now, all the best for the future,

Billy H. C. Reid

PS. Good luck with your new project.

Twenty per cent of the children in a certain elementary school were reported to their teachers as showing unusual potential for intellectual growth. The names of these twenty per cent of the children were drawn by means of a table of random numbers, which is to say that the names were drawn out of a hat. Eight months later these unusual or 'magic' children showed significantly greater gains in IQ than did the remaining children who had not been singled out for the teachers' attention. The change in the teachers' expectations regarding the intellectual performance of these allegedly 'special' children had led to an actual change in the intellectual performance of these randomly selected children . . . who were also described as more interesting, as showing greater intellectual curiosity and as happier.

R. Rosenthal & L. Jacobsen *Pygmalion in the Classroom*

In memory of John Price

Our Country's Good was premièred at the Royal Court Theatre, London on 10 September 1988 with the following cast:

Captain Arthur Phillip, RN (Governor-in-Chief of New South Wales)	Ron Cook
Major Robbie Ross, RM	Mark Lambert
Captain David Collins, RM (Advocate General)	Nick Dunning
Captain Watkin Tench, RM	Jude Akuwudike
Captain Jemmy Campbell, RM	Jim Broadbent
Reverend Johnson	Lesley Sharp
Lieutenant George Johnston, RM	Alphonsia Emmanuel
Lieutenant Will Dawes, RM	Linda Bassett
Second Lieutenant Ralph Clark, RM	David Haig
Second Lieutenant William Faddy, RM	Mossie Smith
Midshipman Harry Brewer, RN (Provost Marshal)	Jim Broadbent
An Aboriginal Australian	Jude Akuwudike
John Arscott	Jim Broadbent
Black Caesar	Jude Akuwudike
Ketch Freeman	Mark Lambert
Robert Sideway	Nick Dunning
John Wisehammer	Ron Cook
Mary Brenham	Lesley Sharp
Dabby Bryant	Mossie Smith
Liz Morden	Linda Bassett
Duckling Smith	Alphonsia Emmanuel
Meg Long	Lesley Sharp

Directed by Max Stafford-Clark
Decor Peter Hartwell
Lighting by Jenny Cane
Sound by Bryan Bowen
Fights Terry King

The play takes place in Sydney, Australia in 1788/9

Act One

Act Two

Left to right: Ralph, Dabby, Mary. Act One, Scene Five: An Audition. Dabby Bryant comes on with a shrinking Mary Brenham in tow

Left to right: Governor Arthur Phillip, Reverend Johnson, Second Lieutenant Ralph Clark, Judge David Collins, Lieutenant George Johnston. Act One, Scene Six: The Authorities Discuss the Merits of the Theatre

Dabby and Mary. Act One, Scene Eight:
The Women Learn Their Lines

Wisehammer and Mary. Act One, Scene Ten:
John Wisehammer and Mary Brenham Exchange Words

Left to right: Ketch Freeman, Sideway and Ralph. Act One, Scene Eleven: The First Rehearsal

Left to right: Ketch Freeman, Black Caesar, Ralph and Duckling. Act One, Scene Eleven: The First Rehearsal

Left to right: Mary, Duckling, Sideway, Arscott, Caesar and, in front, Wisehammer and Liz. Act Two, Scene One: Visiting Hours

Ralph and Governor Phillip. Act Two, Scene Two: His Excellency Exhorts Ralph

Left to right: Major Ross, Ralph, Sideway and Captain Campbell.
Act Two, Scene Five: The Second Rehearsal. One hundred lashes
on the Sirius for answering an officer

Wisehammer, Mary, Ralph. Act Two, Scene Seven:
The Meaning of Plays

Mary and Ralph. Act Two, Scene Nine: A Love Scene

Liz Morden. Act Two, Scene Ten: The Question of Liz

Act One

Scene One

The Voyage Out

The hold of a convict ship bound for Australia, 1787. The convicts huddle together in the semi-darkness. On deck, the convict **Robert Sideway** *is being flogged.* **Second Lieutenant Ralph Clark** *counts the lashes in a barely audible, slow and monotonous voice.*

Ralph Clark Forty-four, forty-five, forty-six, forty-seven, forty-eight, forty-nine, fifty.

Sideway *is untied and dumped with the rest of the convicts. He collapses. No one moves. A short silence.*

John Wisehammer At night? The sea cracks against the ship. Fear whispers, screams, falls silent, hushed. Spewed from our country, forgotten, bound to the dark edge of the earth, at night what is there to do but seek English cunt, warm, moist, soft, oh the comfort, the comfort of the lick, the thrust into the nooks, the crannies of the crooks of England. Alone, frightened, nameless in this stinking hole of hell, take me, take me inside you, whoever you are. Take me, my comfort and we'll remember England together.

John Arscott Hunger. Funny. Doesn't start in the stomach, but in the mind. A picture flits in and out of a corner. Something you've eaten long ago. Roast beef with salt and grated horseradish.

Mary I don't know why I did it. Love, I suppose.

Scene Two

A lone Aboriginal Australian describes the arrival of the First Convict Fleet in Botany Bay on January 20, 1788

The Aborigine A giant canoe drifts onto the sea, clouds billowing from upright oars. This is a dream which has lost its way. Best to leave it alone.

Scene Three

Punishment

Sydney Cove. **Governor Arthur Phillip, Judge David Collins, Captain Watkin Tench, Midshipman Harry Brewer.** *The men are shooting birds.*

Phillip Was it necessary to cross fifteen thousand miles of ocean to erect another Tyburn?

Tench I should think it would make the convicts feel at home.

Collins This land is under English law. The court found them guilty and sentenced them accordingly. There: a bald-eyed corella.

Phillip But hanging?

Collins Only the three who were found guilty of stealing from the colony's stores. And that, over there on the Eucalyptus, is a flock of 'cacatua galerita' – the sulphur-crested cockatoo. You have been made Governor-in-Chief of a paradise of birds, Arthur.

Phillip And I hope not of a human hell, Davey. Don't shoot yet, Watkin, let's observe them. Could we not be more humane?

Tench Justice and humaneness have never gone hand in hand. The law is not a sentimental comedy.

Phillip I am not suggesting they go without punishment. It is the spectacle of hanging I object to. The convicts will feel nothing has changed and will go back to their old ways.

Tench The convicts never left their old ways, Governor, nor do they intend to.

Phillip Three months is not long enough to decide that. You're speaking too loud, Watkin.

Collins I commend your endeavour to oppose the baneful influence of vice with the harmonising arts of civilisation, Governor, but I suspect your edifice will collapse without the mortar of fear.

Phillip Have these men lost all fear of being flogged?

Collins John Arscott has already been sentenced to 150 lashes for assault.

Tench The shoulder-blades are exposed at about 100 lashes and I would say that somewhere between 250 and 500 lashes you are probably condemning a man to death anyway.

Collins With the disadvantage that the death is slow, unobserved and cannot serve as a sharp example.

Phillip Harry?

Harry The convicts laugh at hangings, Sir. They watch them all the time.

Tench It's their favourite form of entertainment, I should say.

Phillip Perhaps because they've never been offered anything else.

Tench Perhaps we should build an opera house for the convicts.

Phillip We learned to love such things because they were offered to us when we were children or young men. Surely no one is born naturally cultured? I'll have the gun now.

Collins We don't even have any books here, apart from the odd play and a few Bibles. And most of the convicts can't read, so let us return to the matter in hand, which is the punishment of the convicts, not their education.

Phillip Who are the condemned men, Harry?

Harry Thomas Barrett, age 17. Transported seven years for stealing one ewe sheep.

Phillip Seventeen!

Tench It does seem to prove that the criminal tendency is innate.

Phillip It proves nothing.

Harry James Freeman, age 25, Irish, transported fourteen years for assault on a sailor at Shadwell Dock.

Collins I'm surprised he wasn't hanged in England.

Harry Handy Baker, marine and the thieves' ringleader.

Collins He pleaded that it was wrong to put the convicts and the marines on the same rations and that he could not work on so little food. He almost swayed us.

Tench I do think that was an unfortunate decision. My men are in a ferment of discontent.

Collins Our Governor-in-Chief would say it is justice, Tench, and so it is. It is also justice to hang these men.

Tench The sooner the better, I believe. There is much excitement in the colony about the hangings. It's their theatre, Governor, you cannot change that.

Phillip I would prefer them to see real plays: fine language, sentiment.

Tench No doubt Garrick would relish the prospect of eight months at sea for the pleasure of entertaining a group of criminals and the odd savage.

Phillip I never liked Garrick, I always preferred Macklin.

Collins I'm a Kemble man myself. We will need a hangman.

Phillip Harry, you will have to organise the hanging and eventually find someone who agrees to fill that hideous office.

Phillip *shoots.*

Collins Shot.

Tench Shot.

Harry Shot, Sir.

Collins It is my belief the hangings should take place tomorrow. The quick execution of justice for the good of the colony, Governor.

Phillip The good of the colony? Oh, look! We've frightened a kankaroo.

They look.

All Ah!

Harry There is also Dorothy Handland, 82, who stole a biscuit from Robert Sideway.

Phillip Surely we don't have to hang an 82-year-old woman?

Collins That will be unnecessary. She hanged herself this morning.

Scene Four

The Loneliness of Men

Ralph Clark's *tent. It is late at night.* **Ralph** *stands, composing and speaking his diary.*

Ralph Dreamt, my beloved Alicia, that I was walking with you and that you was in your riding-habit – oh my dear woman when shall I be able to hear from you –

All the officers dined with the Governor – I never heard of any one single person having so great a power vested in him as Captain Phillip has by his commission as Governor-in-Chief of New South Wales – dined on a cold collation but the Mutton which had been killed yesterday morning was full of maggots – nothing will keep 24 hours in this dismal country I find –

Went out shooting after breakfast – I only shot one cockatoo – they are the most beautiful birds –

Major Ross ordered one of the Corporals to flog with a rope Elizabeth Morden for being impertinent to Captain Campbell – the Corporal did not play with her but laid it home which I was very glad to see – she has long been fishing for it –

On Sunday as usual, kissed your dear beloved image a thousand times – was very much frightened by the lightning as it broke very near my tent – several of the convicts have run away.

He goes to his table and writes in his journal.

If I'm not made 1st Lieutenant soon . . .

Harry Brewer *has come in.*

Ralph Harry –

Harry I saw the light in your tent –

Ralph I was writing my journal.

Silence.

Is there any trouble?

Harry No. (*Pause.*) I just came.

Talk, you know. If I wrote a journal about my life it would fill volumes. Volumes. My travels with the Captain – His Excellency now, no less, Governor-in-Chief, power to raise armies, build cities – I still call him plain Captain Phillip. He likes it from me. The war in America and before that, Ralph, my life in London. That would fill a volume on its own. Not what you would call a good life.

Pause.

Sometimes I look at the convicts and I think, one of those could be you, Harry Brewer, if you hadn't joined the navy when you did. The officers may look down on me now, but what if they found out that I used to be an embezzler?

Ralph Harry, you should keep these things to yourself.

Harry You're right, Ralph.

Pause.

I think the Captain suspects, but he's a good man and he looks for different things in a man –

Ralph Like what?

Harry Hard to say. He likes to see something unusual. Ralph, I saw Handy Baker last night.

Ralph You hanged him a month ago, Harry.

Harry He had a rope – Ralph, he's come back.

Ralph It was a dream. Sometimes I think my dreams are real – But they're not.

Harry We used to hear you on the ship, Ralph, calling for your Betsey Alicia.

Ralph Don't speak her name on this iniquitous shore!

Harry Duckling's gone silent on me again. I know it's because of Handy Baker. I saw him as well as I see you. Duckling wants me, he said, even if you've hanged me. At least your poker's danced its last shindy, I said. At least it's young and straight, he said, she likes that. I went for him but he was gone. But he's going to come back, I know it. I didn't want to hang him, Ralph, I didn't.

Ralph He did steal that food from the stores.

Pause.

I voted with the rest of the court those men should be hanged, I didn't know His Excellency would be against it.

Harry Duckling says she never feels anything. How do I know she didn't feel something when she was with him? She thinks I hanged him to get rid of him, but I didn't, Ralph.

Pause.

Do you know I saved her life? She was sentenced to be hanged at Newgate for stealing two candlesticks but I got her name put on the transport lists. But when I remind her of that she says she wouldn't have cared. Eighteen years old, and she didn't care if she was turned off.

Pause.

These women are sold before they're ten. The Captain says we should treat them with kindness.

Ralph How can you treat such women with kindness? Why does he think that?

Harry Not all the officers find them disgusting, Ralph – haven't you ever been tempted?

Ralph Never! (*Pause.*) His Excellency never seems to notice me.

Pause.

He finds time for Davey Collins, Lieutenant Dawes.

Harry That's because Captain Collins is going to write about the customs of the Indians here – and Lieutenant Dawes is recording the stars.

Ralph I could write about the Indians.

Harry He did suggest to Captain Tench that we do
something to educate the convicts, put on a play or
something, but Captain Tench just laughed. He doesn't like
Captain Tench.

Ralph A play? Who would act in a play?

Harry The convicts of course. He is thinking of talking to
Lieutenant Johnston, but I think Lieutenant Johnston wants
to study the plants.

Ralph I read *The Tragedy of Lady Jane Grey* on the ship. It is
such a moving and uplifting play. But how could a whore
play Lady Jane?

Harry Some of those women are good women, Ralph, I
believe my Duckling is good. It's not her fault – if only she
would look at me, once, react. Who wants to fuck a corpse!

Silence.

I'm sorry. I didn't mean to shock you, Ralph, I have shocked
you, haven't I? I'll go.

Ralph Is His Excellency serious about putting on a play?

Harry When the Captain decides something, Ralph.

Ralph If I went to him – no. It would be better if you did,
Harry, you could tell His Excellency how much I like the
theatre.

Harry I didn't know that Ralph, I'll tell him.

Ralph Duckling could be in it, if you wanted.

Harry I wouldn't want her to be looked at by all the men.

Ralph If His Excellency doesn't like *Lady Jane* we could find
something else.

Pause.

A comedy perhaps . . .

Harry I'll speak to him, Ralph. I like you.

Pause.

It's good to talk . . .

Pause.

You don't think I killed him then?

Ralph Who?

Harry Handy Baker.

Ralph No, Harry. You did not kill Handy Baker.

Harry Thank you, Ralph.

Ralph Harry, you won't forget to talk to His Excellency about the play?

Scene Five

An Audition

Ralph Clark, Meg Long. Meg Long *is very old and very smelly. She hovers over* **Ralph.**

Meg We heard you was looking for some women, Lieutenant. Here I am.

Ralph I've asked to see some women to play certain parts in a play.

Meg I can play, Lieutenant, I can play with any part you like. There ain't nothing puts Meg off. That's how I got my name: Shitty Meg.

Ralph The play has four particular parts for young women.

Meg You don't want a young woman for your peculiar, Lieutenant, they don't know nothing. Shut your eyes and I'll play you as tight as a virgin.

Ralph You don't understand, Long. Here's the play. It's called *The Recruiting Officer*.

Meg Oh, I can do that too.

Ralph What?

Meg Recruiting. Anybody you like. (*She whispers.*) You want women: you ask Meg. Who do you want?

Ralph I want to try some out.

Meg Good idea, Lieutenant, good idea. Ha! Ha! Ha!

Ralph Now if you don't mind –

Meg *doesn't move.*

Long!

Meg (*frightened but still holding her ground*) We thought you was a madge cull.

Ralph What?

Meg You know, a fluter, a mollie. (*Impatiently.*) A prissy cove, a girl! You having no she-lag on the ship. Nor here, neither. On the ship maybe you was seasick. But all these months here. And now we hear how you want a lot of women, all at once. Well, I'm glad to hear that, Lieutenant, I am. You let me know when you want Meg, old Shitty Meg.

She goes off quickly and **Robert Sideway** *comes straight on.*

Sideway Ah, Mr Clark.

He does a flourish.

I am calling you Mr Clark as one calls Mr Garrick Mr Garrick, we have not had the pleasure of meeting before.

Ralph I've seen you on the ship.

Sideway Different circumstances, Mr Clark, best forgotten. I was once a gentleman. My fortune has turned. The wheel . . . You are doing a play, I hear, ah, Drury Lane, Mr Garrick,

the lovely Peg Woffington. (*Conspiratorially*.) He was so cruel
to her. She was so pale –

Ralph You say you were a gentleman, Sideway?

Sideway Top of my profession, Mr Clark, pickpocket, born
and bred in Bermondsey. Do you know London, Sir, don't
you miss it? In these my darkest hours, I remember my
happy days in that great city. London Bridge at dawn –
hand on cold iron for good luck. Down Cheapside with the
market traders – never refuse a mince pie. Into St Paul's
churchyard – I do love a good church – and begin work in
Bond Street. There, I've spotted her, rich, plump, not of the
best class, stands in front of the shop, plucking up courage, I
pluck her. Time for coffee until five o'clock and the pinnacle,
the glory of the day: Drury Lane. The coaches, the actors
scuttling, the gentlemen watching, the ladies tittering, the
perfumes, the clothes, the handkerchiefs.

He hands **Ralph** *the handkerchief he has just stolen from him.*

Here, Mr Clark, you see the skill. Ah, Mr Clark, I beg you, I
entreat you, to let me perform on your stage, to let me feel
once again the thrill of a play about to begin. Ah, I see ladies
approaching: our future Woffingtons, Siddons.

Dabby Bryant *comes on, with a shrinking* **Mary Brenham** *in
tow.* **Sideways** *bows.*

Ladies.

I shall await your word of command, Mr Clark, I shall be in
the wings.

Sideway *scuttles off.*

Dabby You asked to see Mary Brenham, Lieutenant. Here
she is.

Ralph Yes – the Governor has asked me to put on a play.
(*To* **Mary**.) You know what a play is?

Dabby I've seen lots of plays, Lieutenant, so has Mary.

Ralph Have you, Brenham?

Mary (*inaudibly.*) Yes.

Ralph Can you remember which plays you've seen?

Mary (*inaudibly.*) No.

Dabby I can't remember what they were called, but I always knew when they were going to end badly. I knew right from the beginning. How does this one end, Lieutenant?

Ralph It ends happily. It's called *The Recruiting Officer*.

Dabby Mary wants to be in your play, Lieutenant, and so do I.

Ralph Do you think you have a talent for acting, Brenham?

Dabby Of course she does, and so do I. I want to play Mary's friend.

Ralph Do you know *The Recruiting Officer*, Bryant?

Dabby No, but in all those plays, there's always a friend. That's because a girl has to talk to someone and she talks to her friend. So I'll be Mary's friend.

Ralph Silvia – that's the part I want to try Brenham for – doesn't have a friend. She has a cousin. But they don't like each other.

Dabby Oh. Mary doesn't always like me.

Ralph The Reverend Johnson told me you can read and write, Brenham?

Dabby She went to school until she was ten. She used to read to us on the ship. We loved it. It put us to sleep.

Ralph Shall we try reading some of the play?

Ralph *hands her the book.* **Mary** *reads silently, moving her lips.*

I meant read it aloud. As you did on the ship. I'll help you, I'll read Justice Balance. That's your father.

Dabby Doesn't she have a sweetheart?

Ralph Yes, but this scene is with her father.

Dabby What's the name of her lover?

Ralph Captain Plume.

Dabby A Captain! Mary!

Ralph Start here, Brenham.

Mary *begins to read.*

Mary 'Whilst there is life there is hope, Sir.'

Dabby Oh, I like that, Lieutenant. This is a good play, I can tell.

Ralph Shht. She hasn't finished. Start again, Brenham, that's good.

Mary 'Whilst there is life there is hope, Sir; perhaps my brother may recover.'

Ralph That's excellent, Brenham, very fluent. You could read a little louder. Now I'll read.

'We have but little reason to expect it. Poor Owen! But the decree is just; I was pleased with the death of my father, because he left me an estate, and now I'm punished with the loss of an heir to inherit mine.'

Pause. He laughs a little.

This is a comedy. They don't really mean it. It's to make people laugh. 'The death of your brother makes you sole heiress to my estate, which you know is about twelve hundred pounds a year.'

Dabby Twelve hundred pounds! It must be a comedy.

Mary 'My desire of being punctual in my obedience requires that you would be plain in your commands, Sir.'

Dabby Well said, Mary, well said.

Ralph I think that's enough. You read very well, Brenham. Would you also be able to copy the play? We have only two copies.

Dabby Course she will. Where do I come in, Lieutenant? The cousin.

Ralph Can you read, Bryant?

Dabby Not those marks in the books, Lieutenant, but I can read other things. I read dreams very well, Lieutenant. Very well.

Ralph I don't think you're right for Melinda. I'm thinking of someone else. And if you can't read . . .

Dabby Mary will read me the lines, Lieutenant.

Ralph There's Rose . . .

Dabby Rose. I like the name. I'll be Rose. Who is she?

Ralph She's a country girl . . .

Dabby I grew up in Devon, Lieutenant. I'm perfect for Rose. What does she do?

Ralph She – well, it's complicated. She falls in love with Silvia.

Mary *begins to giggle but tries to hold it back.*

But it's because she thinks Silvia's a man. And she – they – she sleeps with her. Rose. With Silvia. Euh. Silvia too. With Rose. But nothing happens.

Dabby It doesn't? Nothing?

Dabby *bursts out laughing.*

Ralph Because Silvia is pretending to be a man, but of course she can't –

Dabby Play the flute? Ha! She's not the only one around here. I'll do Rose.

Ralph I would like to hear you.

Dabby I don't know my lines yet, Lieutenant. When I know my lines, you can hear me do them. Come on, Mary –

Ralph I didn't say you could – I'm not certain you're the right – Bryant, I'm not certain I want you in the play.

Dabby Yes you do, Lieutenant. Mary will read me the lines and I, Lieutenant, will read you your dreams.

There's a guffaw. It's **Liz Morden**.

Ralph Ah. Here's your cousin.

There is a silence. **Mary** *shrinks away.* **Dabby** *and* **Liz** *stare at each other, each holding her ground, each ready to pounce.*

Melinda. Silvia's cousin.

Dabby You can't have her in the play, Lieutenant.

Ralph Why not?

Dabby You don't have to be able to read the future to know that Liz Morden is going to be hanged.

Liz *looks briefly at* **Dabby**, *as if to strike, then changes her mind.*

Liz I understand you want me in your play, Lieutenant. Is that it?

She snatches the book from **Ralph** *and strides off.*

I'll look at it and let you know.

Scene Six

The Authorities Discuss the Merits of the Theatre

Governor Arthur Phillip, Major Robbie Ross, Judge David Collins, Captain Watkin Tench, Captain Jemmy Campbell, Reverend Johnson, Lieutenant George

Johnston, Lieutenant Will Dawes, Second Lieutenant Ralph Clark, Second Lieutenant William Faddy.

It is late at night, the men have been drinking, tempers are high. They interrupt each other, overlap, make jokes under and over the conversation but all engage in it with the passion for discourse and thought of eighteenth-century men.

Ross A play! A f –

Revd. Johnson Mmhm.

Ross A frippery frittering play!

Campbell Aheeh, aeh, here?

Ralph (*timidly*) To celebrate the King's birthday, on June the 4th.

Ross If a frigating ship doesn't appear soon, we'll all be struck with stricturing starvation – and you – you – a play!

Collins Not putting on the play won't bring us a supply ship, Robbie.

Ross And you say you want those contumelious convicts to act in this play. The convicts!

Campbell Eh, kev, weh, discipline's bad. Very bad.

Ralph The play has several parts for women. We have no other women here.

Collins Your wife excepted, Reverend.

Revd. Johnson My wife abhors anything of that nature. After all, actresses are not famed for their morals.

Collins Neither are our women convicts.

Revd. Johnson How can they be when some of our officers set them up as mistresses.

He looks pointedly at **Lieutenant George Johnston.**

Ross Filthy, thieving, lying whores and now we have to watch them flout their flitty wares on the stage!

Phillip No one will be forced to watch the play.

Dawes I believe there's a partial lunar eclipse that night. I shall have to watch that. The sky of this southern hemisphere is full of wonders. Have you looked at the constellations?

Short pause.

Ross Constellations. Plays! This is a convict colony, the prisoners are here to be punished and we're here to make sure they get punished. Constellations! Jemmy? Constellations!

He turns to **Jemmy Campbell** *for support.*

Campbell Tss, weh, marines, marines: war, phoo, discipline. Eh? Service – His Majesty.

Phillip We are indeed here to supervise the convicts who are already being punished by their long exile. Surely they can also be reformed?

Tench We are talking about criminals, often hardened criminals. They have a habit of vice and crime. Many criminals seem to have been born that way. It is in their nature.

Phillip Rousseau would say that we have made them that way, Watkin: 'Man is born free, and everywhere he is in chains.'

Revd. Johnson But Rousseau was a Frenchman.

Ross A Frenchman! What can you expect? We're going to listen to a foraging Frenchman now –

Collins He was Swiss actually.

Campbell Eeh, eyeh, good soldiers, the Swiss.

Phillip Surely you believe man can be redeemed, Reverend?

Revd. Johnson By the grace of God and a belief in the true church, yes. But Christ never proposed putting on plays to his disciples. However, he didn't forbid it either. It must depend on the play.

Johnston He did propose treating sinners, especially women who have sinned, with compassion. Most of the convict women have committed small crimes, a tiny theft –

Collins We know about your compassion, not to say passion, for the women convicts, George.

Tench A crime is a crime. You commit a crime or you don't. If you commit a crime, you are a criminal. Surely that is logical? It's like the savages here. A savage is a savage because he behaves in a savage manner. To expect anything else is foolish. They can't even build a proper canoe.

Phillip They can be educated.

Collins Actually, they seem happy enough as they are. They do not want to build canoes or houses, nor do they suffer from greed and ambition.

Faddy (*looking at* **Ralph**) Unlike some.

Tench Which can't be said of our convicts. But really, I don't see what this has to do with a play. It is at most a passable diversion, an entertainment to wile away the hours of the idle.

Campbell Ttts, weh, heh, the convicts, bone idle.

Dawes We're wiling away precious hours now. Put the play on, don't put it on, it won't change the shape of the universe.

Ralph But it could change the nature of our little society.

Faddy Second Lieutenant Clark change society!

Phillip William!

Tench My dear Ralph, a bunch of convicts making fools of themselves, mouthing words written no doubt by some London ass, will hardly change our society.

Ralph George Farquhar was not an ass! And he was from Ireland.

Ross An Irishman! I have to sit there and listen to an Irishman!

Campbell Tss, tt. Irish. Wilde. Wilde.

Revd. Johnson The play doesn't propagate Catholic doctrine, does it, Ralph?

Ralph He was also an officer.

Faddy Crawling for promotion.

Ralph Of the Grenadiers.

Ross Never liked the Grenadiers myself.

Campbell Ouah, pheuee, grenades, pho. Throw and run. Eh. Backs.

Ralph The play is called *The Recruiting Officer*.

Collins I saw it in London I believe. Yes. Very funny if I remember. Sergeant Kite. The devious ways he used to serve his Captain . . .

Faddy Your part, Ralph.

Collins William, if you can't contribute anything useful to the discussion, keep quiet!

Silence.

Revd. Johnson What is the plot, Ralph?

Ralph It's about this recruiting officer and his friend, and they are in love with these two young ladies from Shrewsbury and after some difficulties, they marry them.

Revd. Johnson It sanctions Holy Matrimony then?

Ralph Yes, yes, it does.

Revd. Johnson That wouldn't do the convicts any harm. I'm having such trouble getting them to marry instead of this sordid cohabitation they're so used to.

Ross Marriage, plays, why not a ball for the convicts!

Campbell Euuh. Boxing.

Phillip Some of these men will have finished their sentence in a few years. They will become members of society again, and help create a new society in this colony. Should we not encourage them now to think in a free and responsible manner?

Tench I don't see how a comedy about two lovers will do that, Arthur.

Phillip The theatre is an expression of civilisation. We belong to a great country which has spawned great playwrights: Shakespeare, Marlowe, Jonson, and even in our own time, Sheridan. The convicts will be speaking a refined, literate language and expressing sentiments of a delicacy they are not used to. It will remind them that there is more to life than crime, punishment. And we, this colony of a few hundred will be watching this together, for a few hours we will no longer be despised prisoners and hated gaolers. We will laugh, we may be moved, we may even think a little. Can you suggest something else that will provide such an evening, Watkin?

Dawes Mapping the stars gives me more enjoyment, personally.

Tench I'm not sure it's a good idea having the convicts laugh at officers, Arthur.

Campbell No. Pheeoh, insubordination, heh, ehh, no discipline.

Ross You want this vice-ridden vermin to enjoy themselves?

Collins They would only laugh at Sergeant Kite.

Ralph Captain Plume is a most attractive, noble fellow.

Revd. Johnson He's not loose, is he Ralph? I hear many of these plays are about rakes and encourage loose morals in women. They do get married? Before, that is, before. And for the right reasons.

Ralph They marry for love and to secure wealth.

Revd. Johnson That's all right.

Tench I would simply say that if you want to build a civilisation there are more important things than a play. If you want to teach the convicts something, teach them to farm, to build houses, teach them a sense of respect for property, teach them thrift so they don't eat a week's rations in one night, but above all, teach them how to work, not how to sit around laughing at a comedy.

Phillip The Greeks believed that it was a citizen's duty to watch a play. It was a kind of work in that it required attention, judgement, patience, all social virtues.

Tench And the Greeks were conquered by the more practical Romans, Arthur.

Collins Indeed, the Romans built their bridges, but they also spent many centuries wishing they were Greeks. And they, after all, were conquered by barbarians, or by their own corrupt and small spirits.

Tench Are you saying Rome would not have fallen if the theatre had been better?

Ralph (*very loud*) Why not? (*Everyone looks at him and he continues, fast and nervously.*) In my own small way, in just a few hours, I have seen something change. I asked some of the convict women to read me some lines, these women who behave often no better than animals. And it seemed to me, as one or two – I'm not saying all of them, not at all – but one or two, saying those well-balanced lines of Mr Farquhar, they seemed to acquire a dignity, they seemed – they seemed to lose some of their corruption. There was one, Mary

Brenham, she read so well, perhaps this play will keep her from selling herself to the first marine who offers her bread –

Faddy (*under his breath*) She'll sell herself to him, instead.

Ross So that's the way the wind blows –

Campbell Hooh. A tempest. Hooh.

Ralph (*over them*) I speak about her, but in a small way this could affect all the convicts and even ourselves, we could forget our worries about the supplies, the hangings and the floggings, and think of ourselves at the theatre, in London with our wives and children, that is, we could, euh –

Phillip Transcend –

Ralph Transcend the darker, euh – transcend the –

Johnston Brutal –

Ralph The brutality – remember our better nature and remember –

Collins England.

Ralph England.

A moment.

Ross Where did the wee Lieutenant learn to speak?

Faddy He must have had one of his dreams.

Tench (*over them*) You are making claims that cannot be substantiated, Ralph. It's two hours, possibly of amusement, possibly of boredom, and we will lose the labour of the convicts during the time they are learning the play. It's a waste, an unnecessary waste.

Revd. Johnson I'm still concerned about the content.

Tench The content of a play is irrelevant.

Ross Even if it teaches insubordination, disobedience, revolution?

Collins Since we have agreed it can do no harm, since it might, possibly, do some good, since the only person violently opposed to it is Major Ross for reasons he has not made quite clear, I suggest we allow Ralph to rehearse his play. Does anyone disagree?

Ross I – I –

Collins We have taken your disagreement into account, Robbie.

Campbell Ah, eeh, I – I – (*He stops.*)

Collins Thank you, Captain Campbell. Dawes? Dawes, do come back to earth and honour us with your attention for a moment.

Dawes What? No? Why not? As long as I don't have to watch it.

Collins Johnston?

Johnston I'm for it.

Collins Faddy?

Faddy I'm against it.

Collins Could you tell us why?

Faddy I don't trust the director.

Collins Tench?

Tench Waste of time.

Collins The Reverend, our moral guide, has no objections.

Revd. Johnson Of course I haven't read it.

Tench Davey, this is not an objective summing up, this is typical of your high-handed manner –

Collins (*angrily*) I don't think you're the one to accuse others of a high-handed manner, Watkin.

Phillip Gentlemen, please.

Collins Your Excellency, I believe, is for the play and I myself am convinced it will prove a most interesting experiment. So let us conclude with our good wishes to Ralph for a successful production.

Ross I will not accept this. You willy-wally wobbly words, Greeks, Romans, experiment, to get your own way. You don't take anything seriously, but I know this play – this play – order will become disorder. The theatre leads to threatening theory and you, Governor, you have His Majesty's commission to build castles, cities, raise armies, administer a military colony, not fandangle about with a lewdy play! I am going to write to the Admiralty about this. (*He goes.*)

Phillip You're out of turn, Robbie.

Campbell Aah – eeh – a. Confusion. (*He goes.*)

Dawes Why is Robbie so upset? So much fuss over a play.

Johnston Major Ross will never forgive you, Ralph.

Collins I have summed up the feelings of the assembled company, Arthur, but the last word must be yours.

Phillip The last word will be the play, gentlemen.

Scene Seven

Harry and Duckling Go Rowing

Harry Brewer, **Duckling Smith**. **Harry** *is rowing,* **Duckling** *is sulking.*

Harry It's almost beginning to look like a town. Look, Duckling, there's the Captain's house. I can see him in his garden.

Harry *waves.* **Duckling** *doesn't turn around.*

Sydney. He could have found a better name. Mobsbury.
Lagtown. Duckling Cove, eh?

Harry *laughs*. **Duckling** *remains morose*.

The Captain said it had to be named after the Home
Secretary. The courthouse looks impressive all in brick.
There's Lieutenant Dawes' observatory. Why don't you look,
Duckling?

Duckling *glances, then turns back*.

The trees look more friendly from here. Did you know the
Eucalyptus tree can't be found anywhere else in the world?
Captain Collins told me that. Isn't that interesting?
Lieutenant Clark says the three orange trees on his island are
doing well. It's the turnips he's worried about, he thinks
they're being stolen and he's too busy with his play to go and
have a look. Would you like to see the orange trees,
Duckling?

Duckling *glowers*.

I thought you'd enjoy rowing to Ralph's island. I thought it
would remind you of rowing on the Thames. Look how blue
the water is. Duckling. Say something. Duckling!

Duckling If I was rowing on the Thames, I'd be free.

Harry This isn't Newgate, Duckling.

Duckling I wish it was.

Harry Duckling!

Duckling At least the gaoler of Newgate left you alone and
you could talk to people.

Harry I let you talk to the women.

Duckling (*with contempt*) Esther Abrahams, Mary Brenham!

Harry They're good women.

Duckling I don't have anything to say to those women, Harry. My friends are in the women's camp –

Harry It's not the women you're after in the women's camp, it's the marines who come looking for buttock, I know you, who do you have your eye on now, who, a soldier? Another marine, a Corporal? Who, Duckling, who?

Pause.

You've found someone already, haven't you? Where do you go, on the beach? In my tent, like with Handy Baker, eh? Where, under the trees?

Duckling You know I hate trees, don't be so filthy.

Harry Filthy, you're filthy, you filthy whore.

Pause.

I'm sorry, Duckling, please. Why can't you? – can't you just be with me? Don't be angry. I'll do anything for you, you know that. What do you want, Duckling?

Duckling I don't want to be watched all the time. I wake up in the middle of the night and you're watching me. What do you think I'm going to do in my sleep, Harry? Watching, watching, watching. JUST STOP WATCHING ME.

Harry You want to leave me. All right, go and live in the women's camp, sell yourself to a convict for a biscuit. Leave if you want to. You're filthy, filthy, opening your legs to the first marine –

Duckling Why are you so angry with your Duckling, Harry? Don't you like it when I open my legs wide to you? Cross them over you – the way you like? What will you do when your little Duckling isn't there anymore to touch you with her soft fingertips, Harry, where you like it? First the left nipple and then the right. Your Duckling doesn't want to leave you, Harry.

Harry Duckling . . .

Duckling I need freedom sometimes, Harry.

Harry You have to earn your freedom with good behaviour.

Duckling Why didn't you let them hang me and take my corpse with you, Harry? You could have kept that in chains. I wish I was dead. At least when you're dead, you're free.

Silence.

Harry You know Lieutenant Clark's play?

Duckling *is silent.*

Do you want to be in it?

Duckling *laughs.*

Dabby Bryant is in it too and Liz Morden. Do you want to be in it? You'd rehearse in the evenings with Lieutenant Clark.

Duckling And he can watch over me instead of you.

Harry I'm trying to make you happy, Duckling, if you don't want to –

Duckling I'll be in the play.

Pause.

How is Lieutenant Clark going to manage Liz Morden?

Harry The Captain wanted her to be in it.

Duckling On the ship we used to see who could make Lieutenant Clark blush first. It didn't take long, haha.

Harry Duckling, you won't try anything with Lieutenant Clark, will you?

Duckling With that Mollie? No.

Harry You're talking to me again. Will you kiss your Harry?

They kiss.

I'll come and watch the rehearsals.

Scene Eight

The Women Learn Their Lines

Dabby Bryant *is sitting on the ground muttering to herself with concentration. She could be counting.* **Mary Brenham** *comes on.*

Mary Are you remembering your lines, Dabby?

Dabby What lines? No. I was remembering Devon. I was on my way back to Bigbury Bay.

Mary You promised Lieutenant Clark you'd learn your lines.

Dabby I want to go back. I want to see a wall of stone. I want to hear the Atlantic breaking into the estuary. I can bring a boat into any harbour, in any weather. I can do it as well as the Governor.

Mary Dabby, what about your lines?

Dabby I'm not spending the rest of my life in this flat, brittle burnt-out country. Oh, give me some English rain.

Mary It rains here.

Dabby It's not the same. I could recognise English rain anywhere. And Devon rain, Mary, Devon rain is the softest in England. As soft as your breasts, as soft as Lieutenant Clark's dimpled cheeks.

Mary Dabby, don't!

Dabby You're wasting time, girl, he's ripe for the plucking. You can always tell with men, they begin to walk sideways. And if you don't –

Mary Don't start. I listened to you once before.

Dabby What would you have done without that lanky sailor drooling over you?

Mary I would have been less of a whore.

Dabby Listen, my darling, you're only a virgin once. You can't go to a man and say, I'm a virgin except for this one lover I had. After that, it doesn't matter how many men go through you.

Mary I'll never wash the sin away.

Dabby If God didn't want women to be whores he shouldn't have created men who pay for their bodies. While you were with your little sailor there were women in that stinking pit of a hold who had three men on them at once, men with the pox, men with the flux, men biting like dogs.

Mary But if you don't agree to it, then you're not a whore, you're a martyr.

Dabby You have to be a virgin to be a martyr, Mary, and you didn't come on that ship a virgin. 'A. H. I love thee to the heart', ha, tattooed way up there –

Dabby *begins to lift* **Mary**'s *skirt to reveal a tattoo high up on the inner thigh.* **Mary** *leaps away.*

Mary That was different. That was love.

Dabby The second difficulty with being a martyr is that you have to be dead to qualify. Well, you didn't die, thanks to me, you had three pounds of beef a week instead of two, two extra ounces of cheese.

Mary Which you were happy to eat!

Dabby We women have to look after each other. Let's learn the lines.

Mary You sold me that first day so you and your husband could eat!

Dabby Do you want me to learn these lines or not?

Mary How can I play Silvia? She's brave and strong. She couldn't have done what I've done.

Dabby She didn't spend eight months and one week on a convict ship. Anyway, you can pretend you're her.

Mary No. I have to be her.

Dabby Why?

Mary Because that's acting.

Dabby No way I'm being Rose, she's an idiot.

Mary It's not such a big part, it doesn't matter so much.

Dabby You didn't tell me that before.

Mary I hadn't read it carefully. Come on, let's do the scene between Silvia and Rose. (*She reads.*) 'I have rested but indifferently, and I believe my bedfellow was as little pleased; poor Rose! Here she comes' –

Dabby I could have done something for Rose. Ha! I should play Silvia.

Mary 'Good morrow, my dear, how d'ye this morning?' Now you say: 'Just as I was last night, neither better nor worse for you.'

Liz Morden *comes on.*

Liz You can't do the play without me. I'm in it! Where's the Lieutenant?

Dabby She's teaching me some lines.

Liz Why aren't you teaching me the lines?

Mary We're not doing your scenes.

Liz Well do them.

Dabby You can read. You can read your own lines.

Liz I don't want to learn them on my own.

Liz *thrusts* **Dabby** *away and sits by* **Mary**.

I'm waiting.

Dabby What are you waiting for, Liz Morden, a blind man to buy your wares?

Mary (*quickly*) We'll do the first scene between Melinda and Silvia, all right?

Liz Yea. The first scene.

Mary *gives* **Liz** *the book.*

Mary You start.

Liz *looks at the book.*

You start. 'Welcome to town, cousin Silvia' –

Liz 'Welcome to town, cousin Silvia' –

Mary Go on – 'I envied you' –

Liz 'I envied you' – You read it first.

Mary Why?

Liz I want to hear how you do it.

Mary Why?

Liz Cause then I can do it different.

Mary 'I envied you your retreat in the country; for Shrewsbury, methinks, and all your heads of shires' –

Dabby Why don't you read it? You can't read!

Liz What?

She lunges at **Dabby**.

Mary I'll teach you the lines.

Dabby Are you her friend now, is that it? Mary the holy innocent and thieving bitch –

Liz *and* **Dabby** *seize each other.* **Ketch Freeman** *appears.*

Ketch (*with nervous affability*) Good morning, ladies. And why aren't you at work instead of at each other's throats?

Liz *and* **Dabby** *turn on him.*

Liz I wouldn't talk of throats if I was you, Mr Hangman Ketch Freeman.

Dabby Crap merchant.

Liz Crapping cull. Switcher.

Mary Roper.

Ketch I was only asking what you were doing, you know, friendly like.

Liz Stick to your ropes, my little galler, don't bother the actresses.

Ketch Actresses? You're doing a play?

Liz Better than dancing the Paddington frisk in your arms – noser!

Ketch I'll nose on you, Liz, if you're not careful.

Liz I'd take a leap in the dark sooner than turn off my own kind. Now take your whirligigs out of our sight, we have lines to learn.

Ketch *slinks away as* **Liz** *and* **Dabby** *spit him off.*

Dabby (*after him*) Don't hang too many people, Ketch, we need an audience!

Mary 'Welcome to town, cousin Silvia.' It says you salute.

Liz (*giving a military salute*) 'Welcome to town, cousin – Silvia.'

Scene Nine

Ralph Clark Tries to Kiss His Dear Wife's Picture

Ralph's *tent. Candlelight.* **Ralph** *paces.*

Ralph Dreamt my beloved Betsey that I was with you and that I thought I was going to be arrested.

He looks at his watch.

I hope to God that there is nothing the matter with you my tender Alicia or that of our dear boy –

He looks at his watch.

My darling tender wife I am reading Proverbs waiting till midnight, the Sabbath, that I might kiss your picture as usual.

He takes his Bible and kneels. Looks at his watch.

The Patrols caught three seamen and a boy in the women's camp.

He reads.

'Let thy fountain be blessed: and rejoice with the wife of thy youth.'

Good God what a scene of whoredom is going on there in the women's camp.

He looks at his watch. Gets up. Paces.

Very hot this night.

Captain Shea killed today one of the kankaroos – it is the most curious animal I ever saw.

He looks at his watch.

Almost midnight, my Betsey, the Lord's day –

He reads.

'And behold, there met him a woman with the attire of an
harlot, and subtle of heart.
So she caught him, and kissed him with an impudent face.'

Felt ill with the toothache my dear wife my God what pain.

Reads.

'So she caught him and kissed him with an impudent
face . . .'

I have perfumed my bed with myrrh, aloes, cinnamon –

Sarah McCormick was flogged today for calling the doctor a
c – midnight –

This being Sunday took your picture out of its prison and
kissed it – God bless you my sweet woman.

*He now proceeds to do so. That is, he goes down on his knees and
brings the picture to himself.* **Ketch Freeman** *comes into the tent.*
Ralph *jumps.*

Ketch Forgive me, Sir, please forgive me, I didn't want to
disturb your prayers. I say fifty Hail Mary's myself every
night, and 200 on the days when – I'll wait outside, Sir.

Ralph What do you want?

Ketch I'll wait quietly, Sir, don't mind me.

Ralph Why aren't you in the camp at this hour?

Ketch I should be, God forgive me, I should be. But I'm not.
I'm here. I have to have a word with you, Sir.

Ralph Get back to the camp immediately, I'll see you in the
morning, Ketch.

Ketch Don't call me that, Sir, I beg you, don't call me by
that name, that's what I came to see you about, Sir.

Ralph I was about to go to sleep.

Ketch I understand, Sir, and your soul in peace, I won't take up your time, Sir, I'll be brief.

Pause.

Ralph Well?

Ketch Don't you want to finish your prayers? I can be very quiet. I used to watch my mother, may her poor soul rest in peace, I used to watch her say her prayers, every night.

Ralph Get on with it!

Ketch When I say my prayers I have a terrible doubt. How can I be sure God is forgiving me? What if he will forgive me, but hasn't forgiven me yet? That's why I don't want to die, Sir. That's why I can't die. Not until I am sure. Are you sure?

Ralph I'm not a convict: I don't sin.

Ketch To be sure. Forgive me, Sir. But if we're in God's power, then surely he makes us sin. I was given a guardian angel when I was born, like all good Catholics, why didn't my guardian angel look after me better? But I think he must've stayed in Ireland. I think the devil tempted my mother to London and both our guardian angels stayed behind. Have you ever been to Ireland, Sir? It's a beautiful country. If I'd been an angel I wouldn't have left it either. And when we came within six fields of Westminister, the devils took over. But it's God's judgement I'm frightened of. And the women's. They're so hard. Why is that?

Ralph Why have you come here?

Ketch I'm coming to that, Sir.

Ralph Hurry up, then.

Ketch I'm speaking as fast as I can, Sir –

Ralph Ketch –

Ketch James, Sir, James, Daniel, Patrick, after my three
uncles. Good men they were too, didn't go to London. If my
mother hadn't brought us to London, may God give peace to
her soul and breathe pity into the hearts of hard women –
because the docks are in London and if I hadn't worked on
the docks, on that day, May 23rd, 1785, do you remember it,
Sir? Shadwell Dock. If only we hadn't left, then I wouldn't
have been there, then nothing would have happened, I
wouldn't have become a coal heaver on Shadwell Dock and
been there on the 23rd of May when we refused to unload
because they were paying us so badly, Sir. I wasn't even near
the sailor who got killed. He shouldn't have done the
unloading, that was wrong of the sailors, but I didn't kill
him, maybe one blow, not to look stupid, you know, just to
show I was with the lads, even if I wasn't, but I didn't kill
him. And they caught five at random, Sir, and I was among
the five, and they found the cudgel, but I just had that to
look good, that's all, and when they said to me later you can
hang or you can give the names, what was I to do, what
would you have done, Sir?

Ralph I wouldn't have been in that situation, Freeman.

Ketch To be sure, forgive me, Sir. I only told on the ones I
saw, I didn't tell anything that wasn't true, death is a
horrible thing, that poor sailor.

Ralph Freeman, I'm going to go to bed now –

Ketch I understand, Sir, I understand. And when it
happened again, here! And I had hopes of making a good life
here. It's because I'm so friendly, see, so I go along, and then
I'm the one who gets caught. That theft, I didn't do it, I was
just there, keeping a look out, just to help some friends, you
know. But when they say to you, hang or be hanged, what do
you do? Someone has to do it. I try to do it well. God had
mercy on the whore, the thief, the lame, surely he'll forgive
the hang – it's the women – they're without mercy – not like
you and me, Sir, men. What I wanted to say, Sir, is that I
heard them talking about the play.

Pause.

Some players came into our village once. They were loved like the angels, Lieutenant, like the angels. And the way the women watched them – the light of a spring dawn in their eyes.

Lieutenant –

I want to be an actor.

Scene Ten

John Wisehammer and Mary Brenham Exchange Words

Mary *is copying* The Recruiting Officer *in the afternoon light.* **John Wisehammer** *is carrying bricks and piling them to one side. He begins to hover over her.*

Mary 'I would rather counsel than command; I don't propose this with the authority of a parent, but as the advice of your friend' –

Wisehammer Friend. That's a good word. Short, but full of promise.

Mary 'That you would take the coach this moment and go into the country.'

Wisehammer Country can mean opposite things. It renews you with trees and grass, you go rest in the country, or it crushes you with power: you die for your country, your country doesn't want you, you're thrown out of your country.

Pause.

I like words.

Pause.

My father cleared the houses of the dead to sell the old
clothes to the poor houses by the Thames. He found a
dictionary – Johnson's dictionary – it was as big as a Bible.
It went from A to L. I started with the A's. Abecedarian:
someone who teaches the alphabet or rudiments of literature.
Abject: a man without hope.

Mary What does indulgent mean?

Wisehammer How is it used?

Mary (*reads*) 'You have been so careful, so indulgent to me' –

Wisehammer It means ready to overlook faults.

Pause.

You have to be careful with words that begin with 'in'. It can
turn everything upside down. Injustice. Most of that word is
taken up with justice, but the 'in' twists it inside out and
makes it the ugliest word in the English language.

Mary Guilty is an uglier word.

Wisehammer Innocent ought to be a beautiful word, but it
isn't, it's full of sorrow. Anguish.

Mary *goes back to her copying.*

Mary I don't have much time. We start this in a few days.

Wisehammer *looks over her shoulder.*

I have the biggest part.

Wisehammer You have a beautiful hand.

Mary There is so much to copy. So many words.

Wisehammer I can write.

Mary Why don't you tell Lieutenant Clark? He's doing it.

Wisehammer No . . . no . . . I'm –

Mary Afraid?

Wisehammer Diffident.

Mary I'll tell him. Well, I won't. My friend Dabby will.
She's –

Wisehammer Bold.

Pause.

Shy is not a bad word, it's soft.

Mary But shame is a hard one.

Wisehammer Words with two L's are the worst. Lonely,
loveless.

Mary Love is a good word.

Wisehammer That's because it only has one L. I like words
with one L: Luck. Latitudinarian.

Mary *laughs.*

Laughter.

Scene Eleven

The First Rehearsal

**Ralph Clark, Robert Sideway, John Wisehammer, Mary
Brenham, Liz Morden, Dabby Bryant, Duckling Smith,
Ketch Freeman.**

Ralph Good afternoon, ladies and gentlemen –

Dabby We're ladies now. Wait till I tell my husband I've
become a lady.

Mary Sshht.

Ralph It is with pleasure that I welcome you –

Sideway Our pleasure, Mr Clark, our pleasure.

Ralph We have many days of hard word ahead of us.

Liz Work! I'm not working. I thought we was acting.

Ralph Now, let me introduce the company –

Dabby We've all met before, Lieutenant, you could say we know each other, you could say we'd know each other in the dark.

Sideway It's a theatrical custom, the company is formally introduced to each other, Mrs Bryant.

Dabby Mrs Bryant? Who's Mrs Bryant?

Sideway It's the theatrical form of address, Madam. You may call me Mr Sideway.

Ralph If I may proceed –

Ketch Shhh! You're interrupting the director.

Dabby So we are, Mr Hangman.

The women all hiss and spit at **Ketch**.

Ralph The ladies first: Mary Brenham who is to play Silvia. Liz Morden who is to play Melinda. Duckling Smith who is to play Lucy, Melinda's maid.

Duckling I'm not playing Liz Morden's maid.

Ralph Why not?

Duckling I live with an officer. He wouldn't like it.

Dabby Just because she lives chained up in that old toss pot's garden.

Duckling Don't you dare talk of my Harry –

Ralph You're not playing Morden's maid, Smith, you're playing Melinda's. And Dabby Bryant, who is to play Rose, a country girl.

Dabby From Devon.

Duckling (*to* **Dabby**) Screw jaws!

Dabby (*to* **Duckling**) Salt bitch!

Ralph That's the ladies. Now, Captain Plume will be played by Henry Kable.

He looks around.

Who seems to be late. That's odd. I saw him an hour ago and he said he was going to your hut to learn some lines, Wisehammer?

Wisehammer *is silent.*

Sergeant Kite is to be played by John Arscott, who did send a message to say he would be kept at work an extra hour.

Dabby An hour! You won't see him in an hour!

Liz (*under her breath*) You're not the only one with new wrinkles in your arse, Dabby Bryant.

Ralph Mr Worthy will be played by Mr Sideway.

Sideway *takes a vast bow.*

Sideway I'm here.

Ralph Justice Balance by James Freeman.

Duckling No way I'm doing a play with a hangman. The words would stick in my throat.

More hisses and spitting. **Ketch** *shrinks.*

Ralph You don't have any scenes with him, Smith. Now if I could finish the introductions. Captain Brazen is to be played by John Wisehammer.

The small parts are still to be cast. Now. We can't do the first scene until John Arscott appears.

Dabby There won't be a first scene.

Ralph Bryant, will you be quiet please! The second scene. Wisehammer, you could read Plume.

Wisehammer *comes forward eagerly.*

No, I'll read Plume myself. So, Act One, Scene Two, Captain Plume and Mr Worthy.

Sideway That's me. I'm at your command.

Ralph The rest of you can watch and wait for your scenes. Perhaps we should begin by reading it.

Sideway No need, Mr Clark. I know it.

Ralph Ah, I'm afraid I shall have to read Captain Plume.

Sideway I know that part too. Would you like me to do both?

Ralph I think it's better if I do it. Shall we begin? Kite, that's John Arscott, has just left –

Dabby Running.

Ralph Bryant! I'll read the line before Worthy's entrance: 'None at present. 'Tis indeed the picture of Worthy, but the life's departed.' Sideway? Where's he gone?

Sideway *has scuttled off. He shouts from the wings.*

Sideway I'm preparing my entrance, Mr Clark, I won't be a minute. Could you read the line again, slowly?

Ralph ''Tis indeed the picture of Worthy, but the life's departed. What, arms-a-cross, Worthy!'

Sideway *comes on, walking sideways, arms held up in a grandiose eighteenth-century theatrical pose. He suddenly stops.*

Sideway Ah, yes, I forgot. Arms-a-cross. I shall have to start again.

He goes off again and shouts.

Could you read the line again louder please?

Ralph 'What, arms-a-cross, Worthy!'

Sideway *rushes on.*

Sideway My wiper! Someone's buzzed my wiper! There's a wipe drawer in this crew, Mr Clark.

Ralph What's the matter?

Sideway There's a pickpocket in the company.

Dabby Talk of the pot calling the kettle black.

Sideway *stalks around the company threateningly.*

Sideway My handkerchief. Who prigged my handkerchief?

Ralph I'm sure it will turn up, Sideway, let's go on.

Sideway I can't do my entrance without my handkerchief. (*Furious.*) I've been practising it all night. If I get my mittens on the rum diver I'll –

He lunges at **Liz**, *who fights back viciously. They jump apart, each taking threatening poses and* **Ralph** *intervenes with speed.*

Ralph Let's assume Worthy has already entered, Sideway. Now, I say: 'What arms-a-cross, Worthy! Methinks you should hold 'em open when a friend's so near. I must expel this melancholy spirit.'

Sideway *has dropped to his knees and is sobbing in a pose of total sorrow.*

What are you doing down there, Sideway?

Sideway I'm being melancholy. I saw Mr Garrick being melancholy once. That is what he did. Hamlet it was.

He stretches his arms to the ground and begins to repeat.

'Oh that this too, too solid flesh would melt. Oh that this too too solid flesh would melt. Oh that this too too – '

Ralph This is a comedy. It is perhaps a little lighter. Try simply to stand normally and look melancholy. I'll say the line again. (**Sideway** *is still sobbing.*) The audience won't hear Captain Plume's lines if your sobs are so loud, Sideway.

Sideway I'm still establishing my melancholy.

Ralph A comedy needs to move quite fast. In fact, I think we'll cut that line and the two verses that follow and go straight to Worthy greeting Plume.

Wisehammer I like the word melancholy.

Sideway A greeting. Yes. A greeting looks like this.

He extends his arms high and wide.

'Plume!' Now I'll change to say the next words. 'My dear Captain', that's affection isn't it? If I put my hands on my heart, like this. Now, 'Welcome'. I'm not quite sure how to do 'Welcome'.

Ralph I think if you just say the line.

Sideway Quite. Now.

He feels **Ralph**.

Ralph Sideway! What are you doing?

Sideway I'm checking that you're safe and sound returned. That's what the line says: 'Safe and sound returned.'

Ralph You don't need to touch him. You can see that!

Sideway Yes, yes. I'll check his different parts with my eyes. Now, I'll put it all together, 'Plume! My dear Captain, welcome. Safe and sound returned!'

He does this with appropriate gestures.

Ralph Sideway – it's a very good attempt. It's very theatrical. But you could try to be a little more – euh – natural.

Sideway Natural! On the stage! But Mr Clark!

Ralph People must – euh – believe you. Garrick after all is admired for his naturalness.

Sideway Of course. I thought I was being Garrick – but never mind. Natural. Quite. You're the director, Mr Clark.

Ralph Perhaps you could look at me while you're saying the lines.

Sideway But the audience won't see my face.

Ralph The lines are said to Captain Plume. Let's move on. Plume says: 'I 'scaped safe from Germany', shall we say – America? It will make it more contemporary –

Wisehammer You can't change the words of the playwright.

Ralph Mm, well, 'and sound, I hope, from London: you see I have – '

Black Caesar *rushes on*.

Ralph Caesar, we're rehearsing – would you –

Caesar I see that well, Monsieur Lieutenant. I see it is a piece of theatre, I have seen many pieces of theatre in my beautiful island of Madagascar so I have decided to play in your piece of theatre.

Ralph There's no part for you.

Caesar There is always a part for Caesar.

Sideway All the parts have been taken.

Caesar I will play his servant.

He stands next to **Sideway**.

Ralph Farquhar hasn't written a servant for Worthy.

Duckling He can have my part. I want to play something else.

Caesar There is always a black servant in a play, Monsieur Lieutenant. And Caesar is that servant. So, now I stand here just behind him and I will be his servant.

Ralph There are no lines for it, Caesar.

Caesar I speak in French. That makes him a more high up gentleman if he has a French servant, and that is good. Now he gets the lady with the black servant. Very chic.

Ralph I'll think about it. Actually, I would like to rehearse the ladies now. They have been waiting patiently and we don't have much time left. Freeman, would you go and see what's happened to Arscott. Sideway, we'll come back to this scene another time, but that was very good, very good. A little, a little euh, but very good.

Sideway *bows out, followed by* **Caesar**.

Now we will rehearse the first scene between Melinda and Silvia. Morden and Brenham, if you would come and stand here. Now the scene is set in Melinda's apartments. Silvia is already there. So, if you stand here, Morden. Brenham, you stand facing her.

Liz (*very, very fast*) 'Welcome to town cousin Silvia I envied you your retreat in the country for Shrewsbury methinks and all your heads of shires are the most irregular places for living – '

Ralph Euh, Morden –

Liz Wait, I haven't finished yet. 'Here we have smoke noise scandal affectation and pretension in short everything to give the spleen and nothing to divert it then the air is intolerable – '

Ralph Morden, you know the lines very well.

Liz Thank you, Lieutenant Clark.

Ralph But you might want to try and act them.

Pause.

Let's look at the scene.

Liz *looks*.

You're a rich lady. You're at home. Now a rich lady would stand in a certain way. Try to stand like a rich lady. Try to look at Silvia with a certain assurance.

Liz Assurance.

Wisehammer Confidence.

Ralph Like this. You've seen rich ladies, haven't you?

Liz I robbed a few.

Ralph How did they behave?

Liz They screamed.

Ralph I mean before you – euh – robbed them.

Liz I don't know. I was watching their purses.

Ralph Have you ever seen a lady in her own house?

Liz I used to climb into the big houses when I was a girl, and just stand there, looking. I didn't take anything. I just stood. Like this.

Ralph But if it was your own house, you would think it was normal to live like that.

Wisehammer It's not normal. It's not normal when others have nothing.

Ralph When acting, you have to imagine things. You have to imagine you're someone different. So, now, think of a rich lady and imagine you're her.

Liz *begins to masticate.*

What are you doing?

Liz If I was rich I'd eat myself sick.

Dabby Me too, potatoes.

The convicts speak quickly and over each other.

Sideway Roast beef and Yorkshire pudding.

Caesar Hearts of palm.

Wisehammer Four fried eggs, six fried eggs, eight fried eggs.

Liz Eels, oysters –

Ralph Could we get on with the scene, please? Brenham, it's your turn to speak.

Mary 'Oh, Madam, I have heard the town commended for its air.'

Liz 'But you don't consider Silvia how long I have lived in't!'

Ralph (*to* **Liz**) I believe you would look at her.

Liz She didn't look at me.

Ralph Didn't she? She will now.

Liz 'For I can assure you that to a lady the least nice in her constitution no air can be good above half a year change of air I take to be the most agreeable of any variety in life.'

Mary 'But prithee, my dear Melinda, don't put on such an air to me.'

Ralph Excellent, Brenham. You could be a little more sharp on the 'don't'.

Mary 'Don't.' (**Mary** *now tries a few gestures.*) 'Your education and mine were just the same, and I remember the time when we never troubled our heads about air, but when the sharp air from the Welsh mountains made our noses drop in a cold morning at the boarding-school.'

Ralph Good! Good! Morden?

Liz 'Our education cousin was the same but our temperaments had nothing alike.'

Ralph That's a little better, Morden, but you needn't be quite so angry with her. Now go on Brenham.

Liz I haven't finished my speech!

Ralph You're right, Morden, please excuse me.

Liz (*embarrassed*) No, no, there's no need for that, Lieutenant. I only meant – I don't have to.

Ralph Please do.

Liz 'You have the constitution of a horse.'

Ralph Much better, Morden. But you must always remember you're a lady. What can we do to help you? Lucy.

Dabby That's you, Duckling.

Ralph See that little piece of wood over there? Take it to Melinda. That will be your fan.

Duckling I'm not fetching nothing for Liz.

Ralph She's not Morden, she's Melinda, your mistress. You're her servant, Lucy. In fact, you should be in this scene. Now take her that fan.

Duckling (*gives the wood to* **Liz**) Here.

Liz Thank you, Lucy, I do appreciate your effort.

Ralph No, you would nod your head.

Wisehammer Don't add any words to the play.

Ralph Now, Lucy, stand behind Morden.

Duckling What do I say?

Ralph Nothing.

Duckling How will they know I'm here? Why does she get all the lines? Why can't I have some of hers?

Ralph Brenham, it's your speech.

Mary 'So far as to be troubled with neither spleen, colic, nor vapours – '

The convicts slink away and sink down, trying to make themselves invisible as **Major Ross**, *followed by* **Captain Campbell**, *come on.*

'I need no salt for my stomach, no – '

She sees the officers herself and folds in with the rest of the convicts.

Ralph Major Ross, Captain Campbell, I'm rehearsing.

Ross Rehearsing! Rehearsing!

Campbell Tssaach. Rehearsing.

Ross Lieutenant Clark is rehearsing. Lieutenant Clark asked us to give the prisoners two hours so he could rehearse, but what has he done with them? What?

Campbell Eeeh. Other things, eh.

Ross Where are the prisoners Kable and Arscott, Lieutenant?

Campbell Eh?

Ralph They seem to be late.

Ross While you were rehearsing, Arscott and Kable slipped into the woods with three others, so five men have run away and it's all because of your damned play and your so-called thespists. And not only have your thespists run away, they've stolen food from the stores for their renegade escapade, that's what your play has done.

Ralph I don't see what the play –

Ross I said it from the beginning. The play will bring down calamity on this colony.

Ralph I don't see –

Ross The devil, Lieutenant, always comes through the mind, here, worms its way, idleness and words.

Ralph Major Ross, I can't agree –

Ross Listen to me, my lad, you're a Second Lieutenant and you don't agree or disagree with Major Ross.

Campbell No discipline, tcchhha.

Ross *looks over the convicts.*

Ross Caesar! He started going with them and came back.

Ralph That's all right, he's not in the play.

Caesar Yes I am, please Lieutenant, I am a servant.

Ross John Wisehammer!

Wisehammer I had nothing to do with it!

Ross You're Jewish, aren't you? You're guilty. Kable was
last seen near Wisehammer's hut. Liz Morden! She was
observed next to the colony's stores late last night in the
company of Kable who was supposed to be repairing the
door. (*To* **Liz**.) Liz Morden, you will be tried for stealing
from the stores. You know the punishment? Death by
hanging. (*Pause*.) And now you may continue to rehearse,
Lieutenant.

Ross *goes*. **Campbell** *lingers, looking at the book*.

Campbell Ouusstta. *The Recruiting Officer*. Good title. Arara.
But a play, tss, a play.

He goes. **Ralph** *and the convicts are left in the shambles of their
rehearsal. A silence*.

Act Two

Scene One

Visiting Hours

Liz, Wisehammer, Arscott, Caesar *all in chains.* **Arscott** *is bent over, facing away.*

Liz Luck? Don't know the word. Shifts its bob when I comes near. Born under a ha'penny planet I was. Dad's a nibbler, don't want to get crapped. Mum leaves. Five brothers, I'm the only titter. I takes in washing. Then. My own father. Lady's walking down the street, he takes her wiper. She screams, he's shoulder-clapped, says, it's not me, Sir, it's Lizzie, look, she took it. I'm stripped, beaten in the street, everyone watching. That night, I take my dad's cudgel and try to kill him, I prig all his clothes and go to my older brother. He don't want me. Liz, he says, why trine for a make, when you can wap for a winne? I'm no dimber mort, I says. Don't ask you to be a swell mollisher, Sister, men want Miss Laycock, don't look at your mug. So I begin to sell my mother of saints. I thinks I'm in luck when I meet the swell cove. He's a bobcull: sports a different wiper every day of the week. He says to me, it's not enough to sell your mossie face, Lizzie, it don't bring no shiners no more. Shows me how to spice the swells. So. Swell has me up the wall, flashes a pocket watch, I lifts it. But one time, I stir my stumps too slow, the swell squeaks beef, the snoozie hears, I'm nibbed. It's up the ladder to rest, I thinks when I goes up before the fortune teller, but no, the judge's a bobcull, I nap the King's pardon and it's seven years across the herring pond. Jesus Christ the hunger on the ship, sailors won't touch me: no rantum scantum, no food. But here, the Governor says, new life. You could nob it here, Lizzie, I thinks, bobcull Gov, this niffynaffy play, not too much work, good crew of rufflers, Kable, Arscott, but no, Ross don't like my mug, I'm nibbed again and now it's up the ladder to rest for good. Well. Lizzie Morden's life. And you, Wisehammer, how did you get here?

Wisehammer Betrayal. Barbarous falsehood. Intimidation. Injustice.

Liz Speak in English, Wisehammer.

Wisehammer I am innocent. I didn't do it and I'll keep saying I didn't.

Liz It doesn't matter what you say. If they say you're a thief, you're a thief.

Wisehammer I am not a thief. I'll go back to England to the snuff shop of Rickett and Loads and say, see, I'm back, I'm innocent.

Liz They won't listen.

Wisehammer You can't live if you think that way.

Pause.

I'm sorry. Seven years and I'll go back.

Liz What do you want to go back to England for? You're not English.

Wisehammer I was born in England. I'm English. What do I have to do to make people believe I'm English?

Liz You have to think English. I hate England. But I think English. And him, Arscott, he's not said anything since they brought him in but he's thinking English, I can tell.

Caesar I don't want to think English. If I think English I will die. I want to go back to Madagascar and think Malagasy. I want to die in Madagascar and join my ancestors.

Liz It doesn't matter where you die when you're dead.

Caesar If I die here, I will have no spirit. I want to go home. I will escape again.

Arscott There's no escape!

Caesar This time I lost my courage, but next time I ask my ancestors and they will help me escape.

Arscott (*shouts*) There's no escape!

Liz See. That's English. You know things.

Caesar My ancestors will know the way.

Arscott There's no escape I tell you.

Pause.

You go in circles out there, that's all you do. You go out there and you walk and walk and you don't reach China. You come back on your steps if the savages don't get you first. Even a compass doesn't work in this foreign upside-down desert. Here. You can read. Why didn't it work? What does it say?

He hands **Wisehammer** *a carefully folded, wrinkled piece of paper.*

Wisehammer It says north.

Arscott Why didn't it work then? It was supposed to take us north to China, why did I end up going in circles?

Wisehammer Because it's not a compass.

Arscott I gave my only shilling to a sailor for it. He said it was a compass.

Wisehammer It's a piece of paper with north written on it. He lied. He deceived you, he betrayed you.

Sideway, Mary *and* **Duckling** *come on.*

Sideway Madam, gentlemen, fellow players, we have come to visit, to commiserate, to offer our humble services.

Liz Get out!

Mary Liz, we've come to rehearse the play.

Wisehammer Rehearse the play?

Duckling The Lieutenant has gone to talk to the Governor. Harry said we could come see you.

Mary The Lieutenant has asked me to stand in his place so we don't lose time. We'll start with the first scene between Melinda and Brazen.

Wisehammer How can I play Captain Brazen in chains?

Mary This is the theatre. We will believe you.

Arscott Where does Kite come in?

Sideway (*bowing to* **Liz**) Madam, I have brought you your fan. (*He hands her the 'fan', which she takes.*)

Scene Two

His Excellency Exhorts Ralph

Phillip, Ralph.

Phillip I hear you want to stop the play, Lieutenant.

Ralph Half of my cast is in chains, Sir.

Phillip That is a difficulty, but it can be overcome. Is that your only reason, Lieutenant?

Ralph So many people seem against it, Sir.

Phillip Are you afraid?

Ralph No, Sir, but I do not wish to displease my superior officers.

Phillip If you break conventions, it's inevitable you make enemies, Lieutenant. This play irritates them.

Ralph Yes and I –

Phillip Socrates irritated the state of Athens and was put to death for it.

Ralph Sir –

Phillip Would you have a world without Socrates?

Ralph Sir, I –

Phillip In the Meno, one of Plato's great dialogues, have you read it, Lieutenant, Socrates demonstrates that a slave boy can learn the principles of geometry as well as a gentleman.

Ralph Ah –

Phillip In other words, he shows that human beings have an intelligence which has nothing to do with the circumstances into which they are born.

Ralph Sir –

Phillip Sit down, Lieutenant. It is a matter of reminding the slave of what he knows, of his own intelligence. And by intelligence you may read goodness, talent, the innate qualities of human beings.

Ralph I see – Sir.

Phillip When he treats the slave boy as a rational human being, the boy becomes one, he loses his fear, and he becomes a competent mathematician. A little more encouragement and he might become an extraordinary mathematician. Who knows? You must see your actors in that light.

Ralph I can see some of them, Sir, but there are others . . . John Arscott –

Phillip He has been given 200 lashes for trying to escape. It will take time for him to see himself as a human being again.

Ralph Liz Morden –

Phillip Liz Morden – (*He pauses.*) I had a reason for asking you to cast her as Melinda. Morden is one of the most difficult women in the colony.

Ralph She is indeed, Sir.

Phillip Lower than a slave, full of loathing, foul mouthed, desperate.

Ralph Exactly, Sir. And violent.

Phillip Quite. To be made an example of.

Ralph By hanging?

Phillip No, Lieutenant, by redemption.

Ralph The Reverend says he's given up on her, Sir.

Phillip The Reverend's an ass, Lieutenant. I am speaking of redeeming her humanity.

Ralph I am afraid there may not be much there, Sir.

Phillip How do we know what humanity lies hidden under the rags and filth of a mangled life? I have seen soldiers given up for dead, limbs torn, heads cut open, come back to life. If we treat her as a corpse, of course she will die. Try a little kindness, Lieutenant.

Ralph But will she be hanged, Sir?

Phillip I don't want a woman to be hanged. You will have to help, Ralph.

Ralph Sir!

Phillip I had retired from His Majesty's Service, Ralph. I was farming. I don't know why they asked me to rule over this colony of wretched souls, but I will fulfil my responsibility. No one will stop me.

Ralph No, Sir, but I don't see –

Phillip What is a statesman's responsibility? To ensure the rule of law. But the citizens must be taught to obey that law of their own will. I want to rule over responsible human beings, not tyrannise over a group of animals. I want there to be a contract between us, not a whip on my side, terror and hatred on theirs. And you must help me, Ralph.

Ralph Yes, Sir. The play –

Phillip Won't change much, but it is the diagram in the sand that may remind – just remind the slave boy – Do you understand?

Ralph I think so.

Phillip We may fail. I may have a mutiny on my hands. They are trying to convince the Admiralty that I am mad.

Ralph Sir!

Phillip And they will threaten you. You don't want to be a Second Lieutenant all your life.

Ralph No, Sir!

Phillip I cannot go over the head of Major Ross in the matter of promotion.

Ralph I see.

Phillip But we have embarked, Ralph, we must stay afloat. There is a more serious threat and it may capsize us all. If a ship does not come within three months, the supplies will be exhausted. In a month, I will cut the rations again. (*Pause.*) Harry is not well. Can you do something? Good luck with the play, Lieutenant. Oh, and Ralph –

Ralph Sir –

Phillip Unexpected situations are often matched by unexpected virtues in people, are they not?

Ralph I believe they are, Sir.

Phillip A play is a world in itself, a tiny colony we could almost say.

Pause.

And you are in charge of it. That is a great responsibility.

Ralph I will lay down my life if I have to, Sir.

Phillip I don't think it will come to that, Lieutenant. You need only do your best.

Ralph Yes, Sir, I will, Sir.

Phillip Excellent.

Ralph It's a wonderful play, Sir. I wasn't sure at first, as you know, but now –

Phillip Good, Good. I shall look forward to seeing it. I'm sure it will be a success.

Ralph Thank you, Sir. Thank you.

Scene Three

Harry Brewer Sees the Dead

Harry Brewer's *tent.* **Harry** *sits, drinking rum, speaking in the different voices of his tormenting ghosts and answering in his own.*

Harry Duckling! Duckling! 'She's on the beach, Harry, waiting for her young Handy Baker.' Go away, Handy, go away! 'The dead never go away, Harry. You thought you'd be the only one to dance the buttock ball with your trull, but no one owns a whore's cunt, Harry, you rent.' I didn't hang you. 'You wanted me dead.' I didn't. 'You wanted me hanged.' All right, I wanted you hanged. Go away! (*Pause.*) 'Death is horrible, Mr Brewer, it's dark, there's nothing.' Thomas Barrett! You were hanged because you stole from the stores. 'I was seventeen, Mr Brewer.' You lived a very wicked life. 'I didn't.' That's what you said that morning, 'I have led a very wicked life.' 'I had to say something, Mr Brewer, and make sense of dying. I'd heard the Reverend say we were all wicked, but it was horrible, my body hanging, my tongue sticking out.' You shouldn't have stolen that food! 'I wanted to live, go back to England, I'd only be twenty-four. I hadn't done it much, not like you.' Duckling! 'I wish I wasn't dead, Mr Brewer I had plans. I was going to have my farm, drink with friends and feel the strong legs of a girl around me – ' You shouldn't have stolen. 'Didn't you ever steal?' No! Yes. But that was different. Duckling! 'Why should you be alive after what you've done?' Duckling! Duckling!

Duckling *rushes on.*

Duckling What's the matter, Harry?

Harry I'm seeing them.

Duckling Who?

Harry All of them. The dead. Help me.

Duckling I heard your screams from the beach. You're having another bad dream.

Harry No. I see them.

Pause.

Let me come inside you.

Duckling Now?

Harry Please.

Duckling Will you forget your nightmares?

Harry Yes.

Duckling Come then.

Harry Duckling . . .

She lies down and lifts her skirts. He begins to go down over her and stops.

What were you doing on the beach? You were with him, he told me, you were with Handy Baker.

Scene Four

The Aborigine Muses on the Nature of Dreams

The Aborigine Some dreams lose their way and wander over the earth, lost. But this is a dream no one wants. It has stayed. How can we befriend this crowded, hungry and disturbed dream?

Scene Five

The Second Rehearsal

Ralph Clark, **Mary Brenham** and **Robert Sideway** are waiting. **Major Ross** and **Captain Campbell** bring the three prisoners **Caesar**, **Wisehammer** and **Liz Morden**. They are still in chains. **Ross** shoves them forward.

Ross Here is some of your caterwauling cast, Lieutenant.

Campbell The Governor, chhht, said, release, tssst. Prisoners.

Ross Unchain Wisehammer and the savage, Captain Campbell. (Points to **Liz**.) She stays in chains. She's being tried tomorrow, we don't want her sloping off.

Ralph I can't rehearse with one of my players in chains, Major.

Campbell Eeh. Difficult. Mmmm.

Ross We'll tell the Governor you didn't need her and take her back to prison.

Ralph No. We shall manage. Sideway, go over the scene you rehearsed in prison with Melinda, please.

Caesar I'm in that scene too, Lieutenant.

Ralph No you're not.

Liz and **Sideway** Yes he is, Lieutenant.

Sideway He's my servant.

Ralph *nods and* **Liz**, **Sideway** *and* **Caesar** *move to the side and stand together, ready to rehearse, but waiting.*

Ralph The rest of us will go from Silvia's entrance as Wilful. Where's Arscott?

Ross We haven't finished with Arscott yet, Lieutenant.

Campbell Punishment, eeeh, for escape. Fainted. Fifty-three lashes left. Heeeh.

Ross (*pointing to* **Caesar**) Caesar's next. After Morden's trial.

Caesar *cringes*.

Ralph Brenham, are you ready? Wisehammer? I'll play Captain Plume.

Ross The wee Lieutenant wants to be in the play too. He wants to be promoted to convict. We'll have you in the chain gang soon, Mr Clark, haha. (*A pause.* **Ross** *and* **Campbell** *stand, watching. The* **Convicts** *are frozen.*)

Ralph Major, we will rehearse now.

Pause. No one moves.

We wish to rehearse.

Ross No one's stopping you, Lieutenant.

Silence.

Ralph Major, rehearsals need to take place in the utmost euh – privacy, secrecy you might say. The actors are not yet ready to be seen by the public.

Ross Not ready to be seen?

Ralph Major, there is a modesty attached to the process of creation which must be respected.

Ross Modesty? Modesty! Sideway, come here.

Ralph Major. Sideway – stay –

Ross Lieutenant, I would not try to countermand the orders of a superior officer.

Campbell Obedience. Ehh, first euh, rule.

Ross Sideway.

Sideway *comes up to* **Ross**.

Take your shirt off.

Sideway *obeys*. **Ross** *turns him and shows his scarred back to the company*.

One hundred lashes on the Sirius for answering an officer. Remember, Sideway? Three hundred lashes for trying to strike the same officer.

I have seen the white of this animal's bones, his wretched blood and reeky convict urine have spilled on my boots and he's feeling modest? Are you feeling modest, Sideway?

He shoves **Sideway** *aside*.

Modesty.

Bryant. Here.

Dabby *comes forward*.

On all fours.

Dabby *goes down on all fours*.

Now wag your tail and bark, and I'll throw you a biscuit. What? You've forgotten? Isn't that how you begged for your food on the ship? Wag your tail, Bryant, bark! We'll wait.

Brenham.

Mary *comes forward*.

Where's your tattoo, Brenham? Show us. I can't see it. Show us.

Mary *tries to obey, lifting her skirt a little.*

If you can't manage, I'll help you. (**Mary** *lifts her skirt a little higher.*) I can't see it.

But **Sideway** *turns to* **Liz** *and starts acting, boldly, across the room, across everyone.*)

Sideway 'What pleasures I may receive abroad are indeed uncertain; but this I am sure of, I shall meet with less cruelty among the most barbarous nations than I have found at home.'

Liz 'Come, Sir, you and I have been jangling a great while; I fancy if we made up our accounts, we should the sooner come to an agreement.'

Sideway 'Sure, Madam, you won't dispute your being in my debt – my fears, sighs, vows, promises, assiduities, anxieties, jealousies, have run on for a whole year, without any payment.'

Campbell Mmhem, good, that. Sighs, vows, promises, hehem, mmm. Anxieties.

Ross Captain Campbell, start Arscott's punishment.

Campbell *goes.*

Liz 'A year! Oh Mr Worthy, what you owe to me is not to be paid under a seven years' servitude. How did you use me the year before – '

The shouts of **Arscott** *are heard.*

'How did you use me the year before – '

She loses her lines. **Sideway** *tries to prompt her.*

Sideway 'When taking advantage – '

Liz 'When taking the advantage of my innocence and necessity – '

But she stops and drops down, defeated. Silence, except for the beating and **Arscott**'s *cries.*

Scene Six

The Science of Hanging

Harry, **Ketch Freeman**, **Liz**, *sitting, staring straight ahead of her.*

Ketch I don't want to do this.

Harry Get on with it, Freeman.

Ketch (*to* **Liz**) I have to measure you.

Pause.

I'm sorry.

Liz *doesn't move.*

You'll have to stand, Liz.

Liz *doesn't move.*

Please.

Pause.

I won't hurt you. I mean, now. And if I have the measurements right, I can make it quick. Very quick. Please.

Liz *doesn't move.*

She doesn't want to get up, Mr Brewer. I could come back later.

Harry Hurry up.

Ketch I can't. I can't measure her unless she gets up. I have to measure her to judge the drop. If the rope's too short, it won't hang her and if the rope is too long, it could pull her head off. It's very difficult, Mr Brewer, I've always done my best.

Pause.

But I've never hung a woman.

Harry (*in* **Tom Barrett**'s *voice*) 'You've hung a boy.' (*To* **Ketch**.) You've hung a boy.

Ketch That was a terrible mess, Mr Brewer, don't you remember. It took twenty minutes and even then he wasn't dead. Remember how he danced and everyone laughed. I don't want to repeat something like that, Mr Brewer, not now. Someone had to get hold of his legs to weigh him down and then –

Harry Measure her, Freeman!

Ketch Yes, Sir. Could you tell her to get up. She'll listen to you.

Harry (*shouts*) Get up, you bitch.

Liz *doesn't move.*

Get up!

He seizes her and makes her stand.

Now measure her!

Ketch (*measuring the neck, etc., of* **Liz**) The Lieutenant is talking to the Governor again, Liz, maybe he'll change his mind. At least he might wait until we've done the play.

Pause.

I don't want to do this.

I know, you're thinking in my place you wouldn't. But somebody will do it, if I don't, and I'll be gentle. I won't hurt you.

Liz *doesn't move, doesn't look at him.*

It's wrong, Mr Brewer. It's wrong.

Harry (*in* **Tom Barrett***'s voice*) 'It's wrong. Death is horrible.' (*In his own voice to* **Ketch**.) There's no food left in the colony and she steals it and gives it to Kable to run away.

Ketch That's true, Liz, you shouldn't have stolen that food. Especially when the Lieutenant trusted us. That was wrong, Liz. Actors can't behave like normal people, not even like normal criminals. Still, I'm sorry. I'll do my best.

Harry 'I had plans.' (*To* **Ketch**.) Are you finished?

Ketch Yes, yes. I have all the measurements I need. No, one more. I need to lift her. You don't mind, do you, Liz?

He lifts her.

She's so light. I'll have to use a very long rope. The fig tree would be better, it's higher. When will they build me some gallows, Mr Brewer? Nobody will laugh at you, Liz, you won't be shamed, I'll make sure of that.

Harry 'You could hang yourself.' Come on, Freeman. Let's go.

Ketch Goodbye, Liz. You were a very good Melinda. No one will be as good as you.

They begin to go.

Liz Mr Brewer.

Harry 'You wanted me dead.' I didn't. You shouldn't've stolen that food!

Ketch Speak to her, please, Mr Brewer.

Harry What?

Liz Tell Lieutenant Clark I didn't steal the food. Tell him – afterwards. I want him to know.

Harry Why didn't you say that before? Why are you lying now?

Liz Tell the Lieutenant.

Harry 'Another victim of yours, another body. I was so frightened, so alone.'

Ketch Mr Brewer.

Harry 'It's dark. There's nothing.' Get away, get away!

Liz Please tell the Lieutenant.

Harry 'First fear, then a pain at the back of the neck. Then nothing.' I can't see. It's dark. It's dark.

Harry *screams and falls.*

Scene Seven

The Meaning of Plays

The Aborigine Ghosts in a multitude have spilled from the dream. Who are they? A swarm of ancestors comes through unmended cracks in the sky. But why? What do they need? If we can satisfy them, they will go back. How can we satisfy them?

Mary, Ralph, Dabby, Wisehammer, Arscott. Mary *and* **Ralph** *are rehearsing. The others are watching.*

Ralph 'For I swear, Madam, by the honour of my profession, that whatever dangers I went upon, it was with the hope of making myself more worthy of your esteem, and if I ever had thoughts of preserving my life, 'twas for the pleasure of dying at your feet.'

Mary 'Well, well, you shall die at my feet, or where you will; but you know, Sir, there is a certain will and testament to be made beforehand.'

I don't understand why Silvia has asked Plume to make a will.

Dabby It's a proof of his love, he wants to provide for her.

Mary A will is a proof of love?

Wisehammer No. She's using will in another sense. He must show his willingness to marry her. Dying is used in another sense, too.

Ralph He gives her his will to indicate that he intends to take care of her.

Dabby That's right, Lieutenant, marriage is nothing, but will you look after her?

Wisehammer Plume is too ambitious to marry Silvia.

Mary If I had been Silvia, I would have trusted Plume.

Dabby When dealing with men, always have a contract.

Mary Love is a contract.

Dabby Love is the barter of perishable goods. A man's word for a woman's body.

Wisehammer Dabby is right. If a man loves a woman, he should marry her.

Ralph Sometimes he can't.

Wisehammer Then she should look for someone who can.

Dabby A woman should look after her own interests, that's all.

Mary Her interest is to love.

Dabby A girl will love the first man who knows how to open her legs. She's called a whore and ends up here. I could write scenes, Lieutenant, women with real lives, not these Shrewsbury prudes.

Wisehammer I've written something. The prologue of this play won't make any sense to the convicts: 'In ancient times, when Helen's fatal charms' and so on. I've written another one. Will you look at it, Lieutenant?

Ralph *does so and* **Wisehammer** *takes* **Mary** *aside.*

You mustn't trust the wrong people, Mary. We could make a new life together, here. I would marry you, Mary, think about it, you would live with me, in a house. He'll have to put you in a hut at the bottom of his garden and call you his servant in public, that is, his whore. Don't do it, Mary.

Dabby Lieutenant, are we rehearsing or not? Arscott and I have been waiting for hours.

Ralph It seems interesting, I'll read it more carefully later.

Wisehammer You don't like it.

Ralph I do like it. Perhaps it needs a little more work. It's not Farquhar.

Wisehammer It would mean more to the convicts.

Ralph We'll talk about it another time.

Wisehammer Do you think it should be longer?

Ralph I'll think about it.

Wisehammer Shorter? Do you like the last two lines? Mary helped me with them.

Ralph Ah.

Wisehammer The first lines took us days, didn't they, Mary?

Ralph We'll rehearse Silvia's entrance as Jack Wilful. You're in the scene, Wisehammer. We'll come to your scenes in a minute, Bryant. Now, Brenham, remember what I showed you yesterday about walking like a gentleman? I've ordered breeches to be made for you, you can practise in them tomorrow.

Mary I'll tuck my skirt in. (*She does so and takes a masculine pose.*) 'Save ye, save ye, gentlemen.'

Wisehammer 'My dear, I'm yours.'

He kisses her.

Ralph (*angrily*) It doesn't say Silvia is kissed in the stage directions!

Wisehammer Plume kisses her later and there's the line about men kissing in the army. I thought Brazen would kiss her immediately.

Ralph It's completely wrong.

Wisehammer It's right for the character of Brazen.

Ralph No it isn't. I'm the director, Wisehammer.

Wisehammer Yes, but I have to play the part. They're equal in this scene. They're both Captains and in the end fight for her. Who's playing Plume in our performance?

Ralph I will have to, as Kable hasn't come back. It's your line.

Wisehammer Will I be given a sword?

Ralph I doubt it. Let's move on to Kite's entrance, Arscott has been waiting too long.

Arscott (*delighted, launches straight in*) 'Sir, if you please – '

Ralph Excellent, Arscott, but we should just give you our last lines so you'll know when to come in. Wisehammer.

Wisehammer 'The fellow dare not fight.'

Ralph That's when you come in.

Arscott 'Sir, if you please – '

Dabby What about me? I haven't done anything either. You always rehearse the scenes with Silvia.

Ralph Let's rehearse the scene where Rose comes on with her brother Bullock. It's a better scene for you Arscott. Do you know it?

Arscott Yes.

Ralph Good. Wisehammer, you'll have to play the part of Bullock.

Wisehammer What? Play two parts?

Ralph Major Ross won't let any more prisoners off work. Some of you will have to play several parts.

Wisehammer It'll confuse the audience. They'll think Brazen is Bullock and Bullock Brazen.

Ralph Nonsense, if the audience is paying attention, they'll know that Bullock is a country boy and Brazen a Captain.

Wisehammer What if they aren't paying attention?

Ralph People who can't pay attention should not go to the theatre.

Mary If you act well, they will have to pay attention.

Wisehammer It will ruin my entrance as Captain Brazen.

Ralph We have no choice and we must turn this necessity into an advantage. You will play two very different characters and display the full range of your abilities.

Wisehammer Our audience won't be that discerning.

Ralph Their imagination will be challenged and trained. Let's start the scene. Bryant?

Dabby I think *The Recruiting Officer* is a silly play. I want to be in a play that has more interesting people in it.

Mary I like playing Silvia. She's bold, she breaks rules out of love for her Captain and she's not ashamed.

Dabby She hasn't been born poor, she hasn't had to survive, and her father's a Justice of the Peace. I want to play myself.

Arscott I don't want to play myself. When I say Kite's lines I forget everything else. I forget the judge said I'm going to have to spend the rest of my natural life in this place getting beaten and working like a slave. I can forget that out there it's trees and burnt grass, spiders that kill you in four hours and snakes. I don't have to think about what happened to Kable, I don't have to remember the things I've done, when I speak Kite's lines I don't hate any more. I'm Kite. I'm in Shrewsbury. Can we get on with the scene, Lieutenant, and stop talking?

Dabby I want to see a play that shows life as we know it.

Wisehammer A play should make you understand something new. If it tells you what you already know, you leave it as ignorant as you went in.

Dabby Why can't we do a play about now?

Wisehammer It doesn't matter when a play is set. It's better if it's set in the past, it's clearer. It's easier to understand Plume and Brazen than some of the officers we know here.

Ralph Arscott, would you start the scene?

Arscott 'Captain, Sir, look yonder, a-coming this way, 'tis the prettiest, cleanest, little tit.'

Ralph Now Worthy – He's in this scene. Where's Sideway?

Mary He's so upset about Liz he won't rehearse.

Ralph I am going to talk to the Governor, but he has to rehearse. We must do the play, whatever happens. We've been rehearsing for five months! Let's go on. 'Here she comes, and what is that great country fellow with her?'

Arscott 'I can't tell, Sir.'

Wisehammer I'm not a great country fellow.

Ralph Act it, Wisehammer.

Dabby 'Buy chickens, young and tender, young and tender chickens.' This is a very stupid line and I'm not saying it.

Ralph It's written by the playwright and you have to say it. 'Here, you chickens!'

Dabby 'Who calls?'

Ralph Bryant, you're playing a pretty country wench who wants to entice the Captain. You have to say these lines with charm and euh – blushes.

Dabby I don't blush.

Ralph I can't do this scene without Sideway. Let's do another scene.

Pause.

Arscott, let's work on your big speeches, I haven't heard them yet. I still need Sideway. This is irresponsible, he wanted the part. Somebody go and get Sideway.

No one moves.

Arscott I'll do the first speech anyway, Sir. 'Yes, Sir, I understand my business, I will say it; you must know, Sir, I was born a gypsy, and bred among that crew till I was ten years old, there I learned canting and lying; – '

Dabby That's about me!

Arscott 'I was bought from my mother Cleopatra by a certain nobleman, for three guineas, who liking my beauty made me his page – '

Dabby That's my story. Why do I have to play a silly milkmaid? Why can't I play Kite?

Mary You can't play a man, Dabby.

Dabby You're playing a man: Jack Wilful.

Mary Yes, but in the play, I know I'm a woman, whereas if you played Kite, you would have to think you were a man.

Dabby If Wisehammer can think he's a big country lad, I can think I'm a man. People will use their imagination and people with no imagination shouldn't go to the theatre.

Ralph Bryant, you're muddling everything.

Dabby No. I see things very clearly and I'm making you see clearly, Lieutenant. I want to play Kite.

Arscott You can't play Kite! I'm playing Kite! You can't steal my part!

Ralph You may have to play Melinda.

Dabby All she does is marry Sideway, that's not interesting.

Dabby *stomps off.* **Ketch** *comes on.*

Ketch I'm sorry I'm late, Lieutenant, but I know all my lines.

Ralph We'll rehearse the first scene between Justice Balance and Silvia. Brenham.

Arscott *stomps off.*

Mary 'Whilst there is life there is hope, Sir; perhaps my brother may recover.'

Ketch 'We have but little reason to expect it – '

Mary I can't. Not with him. Not with Liz – I can't.

She runs off.

Ralph One has to transcend personal feelings in the theatre.

Wisehammer *runs after* **Mary**.

(*To* **Ketch**.) We're not making much progress today, let's end this rehearsal.

He goes. **Ketch** *is left alone, bewildered.*

Scene Eight

Duckling Makes Vows

Night. **Harry**, *ill.* **Duckling**.

Duckling If you live, I will never again punish you with my silence. If you live, I will never again turn away from you. If you live, I will never again imagine another man when you make love to me. If you live, I will never tell you I want to leave you. If you live, I will speak to you. If you live, I will be tender with you. If you live, I will look after you. If you live, I will stay with you. If you live, I will be wet and open to your touch. If you live, I will answer all your questions. If you live, I will look at you. If you live, I will love you.

Pause.

If you die, I will never forgive you.

She leans over him. Listens. Touches. **Harry** *is dead.*

I hate you.

No. I love you.

She crouches into a foetal position, cries out.

How could you do this?

Scene Nine

A Love Scene

The beach. Night. **Mary,** *then* **Ralph.**

Mary (*to herself*) 'Captain Plume, I despise your listing-money; if I do serve, 'tis purely for love – of that wench I mean. For you must know,' etc –

'So you only want an opportunity for accomplishing your designs upon her?'

'Well, Sir, I'm satisfied as to the point in debate; but now let me beg you to lay aside your recruiting airs, put on the man of honour, and tell me plainly what usage I must expect when I'm under your command.'

She tries that again, with a stronger and lower voice. **Ralph** *comes on, sees her. She sees him, but continues.*

'And something tells me, that if you do discharge me 'twill be
the greatest punishment you can inflict; for were we this
moment to go upon the greatest dangers in your profession,
they would be less terrible to me than to stay behind you.
And now your hand – this lists me – and now you are my
Captain.'

Ralph (*as* **Plume**) 'Your friend.' (*Kisses her.*) ''Sdeath! There's
something in this fellow that charms me.'

Mary 'One favour I must beg – this affair will make some
noise – '

Ralph Silvia –

He kisses her again.

Mary 'I must therefore take care to be impressed by the Act
of Parliament – '

Ralph 'What you please as to that. Will you lodge at my
quarters in the meantime? You shall have part of my bed.'
Silvia. Mary.

Mary Am I doing it well? It's difficult to play a man. It's not
the walk, it's the way you hold your head. A man doesn't
bow his head so much and never at an angle. I must face you
without lowering my head. Let's try it again.

Ralph 'What you please as to that. – Will you lodge at my
quarters in the meantime? You shall have part of my bed.'
Mary!

She holds her head straight. Pause.

Will you?

Pause.

Mary Yes.

They kiss.

Ralph Don't lower your head. Silvia wouldn't.

She begins to undress, from the top.

I've never looked at the body of a woman before.

Mary Your wife?

Ralph It wasn't right to look at her.
Let me see you.

Mary Yes.
Let me see you.

Ralph Yes.

He begins to undress himself.

Scene Ten

The Question of Liz

Ralph, Ross, Phillip, Collins, Campbell.

Collins She refused to defend herself at the trial. She didn't say a word. This was taken as an admission of guilt and she was condemned to be hanged. The evidence against her, however, is flimsy.

Ross She was seen with Kable next to the food stores. That is a fingering fact.

Collins She was seen by a drunken soldier in the dark. He admitted he was drunk and that he saw her at a distance. He knew Kable was supposed to be repairing the door and she's known to be friends with Kable and Arscott. She won't speak, she won't say where she was. That is our difficulty.

Ross She won't speak because she's guilty.

Phillip Silence has many causes, Robbie.

Ralph She won't speak, Your Excellency, because of the convict code of honour. She doesn't want to beg for her life.

Ross Convict code of honour. This pluming play has muddled the muffy Lieutenant's mind.

Collins My only fear, Your Excellency, is that she may have refused to speak because she no longer believes in the process of justice. If that is so, the courts here will become travesties. I do not want that.

Phillip But if she won't speak, there is nothing more we can do. You cannot get at the truth through silence.

Ralph She spoke to Harry Brewer.

Phillip But Harry never regained consciousness before he died.

Ralph James Freeman was there and told me what she said.

Phillip Wasn't this used in the trial?

Collins Freeman's evidence wasn't very clear and as Liz Morden wouldn't confirm what he said, it was dismissed.

Ross You can't take the word of a crooked crawling hangman.

Phillip Why won't she speak?

Ross Because she's guilty.

Phillip Robbie, we may be about to hang the first woman in this colony. I do not want to hang the first innocent woman.

Ralph We must get at the truth.

Ross Truth! We have 800 thieves, perjurers, forgers, murderers, liars, escapers, rapists, whores, coiners in this scrub-ridden, dust-driven, thunder-bolted, savage-run, cretinous colony. My marines who are trained to fight are turned into gouly gaolers, fed less than the prisoners –

Phillip The rations, Major, are the same for all, prisoners and soldiers.

Ross They have a right to more so that makes them have less. Not a ship shifting into sight, the prisoners running away, stealing, drinking and the wee ductile Lieutenant talks about the truth.

Phillip Truth is indeed a luxury, but its absence brings about the most abject poverty in a civilisation. That is the paradox.

Ross This is a profligate prison for us all, it's a hellish hole we soldiers have been hauled to because they blame us for losing the war in America. This is a hateful, hary-scary, topsy-turvy outpost, this is not a civilisation. I hate this possumy place.

Collins Perhaps we could return to the question of Liz Morden. (*Calls.*) Captain Campbell.

Campbell *brings in* **Liz Morden**.

Morden, if you don't speak, we will have to hang you; if you can defend yourself, His Excellency can overrule the court. We would not then risk a miscarriage of justice. But you must speak. Did you steal that food with the escaped prisoner Kable?

A long silence.

Ralph She –

Collins It is the accused who must answer.

Phillip Liz Morden. You must speak the truth.

Collins We will listen to you.

Pause.

Ralph Morden. No one will despise you for telling the truth.

Phillip That is not so, Lieutenant. Tell the truth and accept the contempt. That is the history of great men. Liz, you may be despised, but you will have shown courage.

Ralph If that soldier has lied –

Ross There, there, he's accusing my soldiers of lying. It's that play, it makes fun of officers, it shows an officer lying and cheating. It shows a corrupt justice as well, Collins –

Campbell Good scene that, very funny, hah, scchhh.

Collins Et tu, Campbell?

Campbell What? Meant only. Hahah. If he be so good at gunning he shall have enough – he may be of use against the French, for he shoots flying, hahaha. Good, and then there's this Constable ha –

Ross Campbell!

Phillip The play seems to be having miraculous effects already. Don't you want to be in it, Liz?

Ralph Morden, you must speak.

Collins For the good of the colony.

Phillip And of the play.

A long silence.

Liz I didn't steal the food.

Collins Were you there when Kable stole it?

Liz No. I was there before.

Ross And you knew he was going to steal it?

Liz Yes.

Ross Guilty. She didn't report it.

Collins Failure to inform is not a hangable offence.

Ross Conspiracy.

Collins We may need a retrial.

Phillip Why wouldn't you say any of this before?

Ross Because she didn't have time to invent a lie.

Collins Major, you are demeaning the process of law.

Phillip Why, Liz?

Liz Because it wouldn't have mattered.

Phillip Speaking the truth?

Liz Speaking.

Ross You are taking the word of a convict against the word of a soldier –

Collins A soldier who was drunk and uncertain of what he saw.

Ross A soldier is a soldier and has a right to respect. You will have revolt on your hands, Governor.

Phillip I'm sure I will, but let us see the play first. Liz, I hope you are good in your part.

Ralph She will be, Your Excellency, I promise that.

Liz Your Excellency, I will endeavour to speak Mr Farquhar's lines with the elegance and clarity their own worth commands.

Scene Eleven

Backstage

Night. **The Aborigine**.

The Aborigine Look: oozing pustules on my skin, heat on my forehead. Perhaps we have been wrong all this time and this is not a dream at all.

The **Actors** *come on. They begin to change and make up.* **The Aborigine** *drifts off.*

Mary Are the savages coming to see the play as well?

Ketch They come around the camp because they're dying: smallpox.

Mary Oh.

Sideway I hope they won't upset the audience.

Mary Everyone is here. All the officers too.

Liz (*to* **Duckling**) Dabby could take your part.

Duckling No. I will do it. I will remember the lines.

Mary I've brought you an orange from Lieutenant Clark's island. They've thrown her out of Harry Brewer's tent.

Wisehammer Why? He wouldn't have wanted that.

Duckling Major Ross said a whore was a whore and I was to go into the women's camp. They've taken all of Harry's things.

She bursts into tears.

Mary I'll talk to the Lieutenant.

Liz Let's go over your lines. And if you forget them, touch my foot and I'll whisper them to you.

Sideway (*who has been practising on his own*) We haven't rehearsed the bow. Garrick used to take his this way: you look up to the circle, to the sides, down, make sure everyone thinks you're looking at them. Get in a line.

They do so.

Arscott I'll be in the middle. I'm the tallest.

Mary No, Arscott. (**Mary** *places herself in the middle.*)

Sideway Dabby, you should be next to Mary.

Dabby I won't take the bow.

Sideway It's not the biggest part, Dabby, but you'll be noticed.

Dabby I don't want to be noticed.

Sideway Let's get this right. If we don't all do the same thing, it will look a mess.

They try. **Dabby** *is suddenly transfixed.*

Dabby Hurray, hurray, hurray.

Sideway No, they will be shouting bravo, but we're not in a line yet.

Dabby I wasn't looking at the bow, I saw the whole play, and we all knew our lines, and Mary, you looked so beautiful, and after that, I saw Devon and they were shouting bravo, bravo Dabby, hurray, you've escaped, you've sailed thousands and thousands of miles on the open sea and you've come back to your Devon, bravo Dabby, bravo.

Mary When are you doing this, Dabby?

Dabby Tonight.

Mary You can't.

Dabby I'll be in the play till the end, then in the confusion, when it's over, we can slip away. The tide is up, the night will be dark, everything's ready.

Mary The Lieutenant will be blamed, I won't let you.

Dabby If you say anything to the Lieutenant, I'll refuse to act in the play.

Arscott When I say my lines, I think of nothing else. Why can't you do the same?

Dabby Because it's only for one night. I want to grow old in Devon.

Mary They'll never let us do another play, I'm telling the Lieutenant.

All No, you're not.

Dabby Please, I want to go back to Devon.

Wisehammer I don't want to go back to England now. It's too small and they don't like Jews. Here, no one has more of a right than anyone else to call you a foreigner. I want to become the first famous writer.

Mary You can't become a famous writer until you're dead.

Wisehammer You can if you're the only one.

Sideway I'm going to start a theatre company. Who wants to be in it?

Wisehammer I will write you a play about justice.

Sideway Only comedies, my boy, only comedies.

Wisehammer What about a comedy about unrequited love?

Liz I'll be in your company, Mr Sideway.

Ketch And so will I. I'll play all the parts that have dignity and gravity.

Sideway I'll hold auditions tomorrow.

Dabby Tomorrow.

Duckling Tomorrow.

Mary Tomorrow.

Liz Tomorrow.

A long silence. (Un ange passe.)

Mary Where are my shoes?

Ralph *comes in.*

Ralph Arscott, remember to address the soldiers when you talk of recruiting. Look at them: you are speaking to them. And don't forget, all of you, to leave a space for people to laugh.

Arscott I'll kill anyone who laughs at me.

Ralph They're not laughing at you, they're laughing at Farquhar's lines. You must expect them to laugh.

Arscott That's all right, but if I see Major Ross or any other officer laughing at me, I'll kill them.

Mary No more violence. By the way, Arscott, when you carry me off the stage as Jack Wilful, could you be a little more gentle? I don't think he'd be so rough with a young gentleman.

Ralph Where's Caesar?

Ketch I saw him walking towards the beach earlier. I thought he was practising his lines.

Arscott Caesar!

He goes out.

Wisehammer (*to* **Liz**) When I say 'Do you love fishing, Madam?', do you say something then? –

Ralph (*goes over to* **Duckling**) I am so sorry, Duckling. Harry was my friend.

Duckling I loved him. But now he'll never know that. I thought that if he knew he would become cruel.

Ralph Are you certain you don't want Dabby to take your part?

Duckling No! I will do it. I want to do it.

Pause.

He liked to hear me say my lines.

Ralph He will be watching from somewhere. (*He goes to* **Mary**.) How beautiful you look.

Mary I dreamt I had a necklace of pearls and three children.

Ralph If we have a boy we will call him Harry.

Mary And if we have a girl?

Ralph She will be called Betsey Alicia.

Arscott *comes in with* **Caesar** *drunk and dishevelled.*

Arscott Lying on the beach, dead drunk.

Caesar (*to* **Ralph**, *pleading*) I can't. All those people. My ancestors are angry, they do not want me to be laughed at by all those people.

Ralph You wanted to be in this play and you will be in this play –

Ketch I'm nervous too, but I've overcome it. You have to be brave to be an actor.

Caesar My ancestors will kill me.

He swoons. **Arscott** *hits him.*

Arscott You're going to ruin my first scene.

Caesar Please, Lieutenant, save me.

Ralph Caesar, if I were back home, I wouldn't be in this play either. My ancestors wouldn't be very pleased to see me here – But our ancestors are thousands of miles away.

Caesar I cannot be a disgrace to Madagascar.

Arscott You will be more of a disgrace if you don't come out with me on that stage. NOW.

Mary Think of us as your family.

Sideway (*to* **Ralph**) What do you think of this bow?

Ralph Caesar, I am your Lieutenant and I command you to go on that stage. If you don't, you will be tried and hanged for treason.

Ketch And I'll tie the rope in such a way you'll dangle there for hours full of piss and shit.

Ralph What will your ancestors think of that, Caesar?

Caesar *cries but pulls himself together.*

Ketch (*to* **Liz**) I couldn't have hanged you.

Liz No?

Ralph Dabby, have you got your chickens?

Dabby My chickens? Yes. Here.

Ralph Are you all right?

Dabby Yes. (*Pause.*) I was dreaming.

Ralph Of your future success?

Dabby Yes. Of my future success.

Ralph And so is everyone here, I hope. Now, Arscott.

Arscott Yes, Sir!

Ralph Calm.

Arscott I have been used to danger, Sir.

Sideway Here.

Liz What's that?

Sideway Salt. For good luck.

Ralph Where did you get that from?

Sideway I have been saving it from my rations. I have saved enough for each of us to have some.

They all take a little salt.

Wisehammer Lieutenant?

Ralph Yes, Wisehammer.

Wisehammer There's – there's –

Mary There's his prologue.

Ralph The prologue. I forgot.

Pause.

Let me hear it again.

Wisehammer
From distant climes o'er wide-spread seas we come,
Though not with much éclat or beat of drum,
True patriots all; for be it understood,
We left our country for our country's good;
No private views disgraced our generous zeal,
What urg'd our travels was our country's weal,
And none will doubt but that our emigration
Has prov'd most useful to the British nation.

Silence.

Ralph When Major Ross hears that, he'll have an apoplectic fit.

Mary I think it's very good.

Dabby So do I. And true.

Sideway But not theatrical.

Ralph It is very good, Wisehammer, it's very well written, but it's too – too political. It will be considered provocative.

Wisehammer You don't want me to say it.

Ralph Not tonight. We have many people against us.

Wisehammer I could tone it down. I could omit 'We left our country for our country's good.'

Dabby That's the best line.

Ralph It would be wrong to cut it.

Wisehammer I worked so hard on it.

Liz It rhymes.

Sideway We'll use it in the Sideway Theatre.

Ralph You will get much praise as Brazen, Wisehammer.

Wisehammer It isn't the same as writing.

Ralph The theatre is like a small republic, it requires private sacrifices for the good of the whole. That is something you should agree with, Wisehammer.

Pause.

And now, my actors, I want to say what a pleasure it has been to work with you. You are on your own tonight and you must do your utmost to provide the large audience out there with a pleasurable, intelligible and memorable evening.

Liz We will do our best, Mr Clark.

Mary I love this!

Ralph Arscott.

Arscott (*to* **Caesar**) You walk three steps ahead of me. If you stumble once, you know what will happen to you later? Move!

Ralph You're on.

Arscott is about to go on, then remembers.

Arscott Halberd! Halberd!

He is handed his halberd and goes upstage and off, preceded by **Caesar** *beating the drum. Backstage, the remaining actors listen with trepidation to* **Kite**'s *first speech.*

Arscott 'If any gentlemen soldiers, or others, have a mind to serve Her Majesty, and pull down the French King; if any prentices have severe masters, any children have undutiful parents; if any servants have too little wages or any husband too much wife; let them repair to the noble Sergeant Kite, at the Sign of the Raven, in this good town of Shrewsbury, and they shall receive present relief and entertainment' . . .

And to the triumphant music of Beethoven's Fifth Symphony *and the sound of applause and laughter from the First Fleet audience, the first Australian performance of* The Recruiting Officer *begins.*

Notes

These notes are intended for use by overseas students as well as by English-born readers. References are to *The Playmaker* by Thomas Keneally, *The Fatal Shore* by Robert Hughes and *The Recruiting Officer* by George Farquhar (New Mermaid Edition).

2   *Tyburn*—the eighteenth-century place of public execution in London, situated at the present junction of Oxford Street and Edgware Road

3   *baneful*—destructive, harmful

4   *Shadwell Dock*—a London dock on the River Thames

5   *Garrick*—David Garrick (1717–79), actor, manager of Drury Lane Theatre, noted for his easy natural manner of speech

5   *Macklin*—Charles Macklin (1700–97), actor, famous for his Shakespeare roles

5   *Kemble*—John Philip Kemble (1757–1823), actor and theatre manager noted for his tragic playing

6   *collation*—meal

6   *made 1st Lieutenant*—Ralph Clark is a lowly Second Lieutenant and keen for promotion

7   *war in America*—The American War of Independence

8   *Newgate*—a celebrated London prison

8   *turned off*—hanged

10   *your peculiar*—mistress

11   *a madge cull, a fluter, a mollie, a prissy cove*—cant terms for a homosexual or an effeminate male

11   *she-lag*—female convict

11   *a flourish*—an ostentatious bow

11   *The wheel*—the wheel of fortune

11   *Drury Lane*—the Theatre Royal, Drury Lane, one of

London's major theatres, opened in 1663. The present
building is the fourth on the site

12 *Peg Woffington*—(1718–60) actress, outstanding in
comedy. She played Sylvia in *The Recruiting Officer* at
Drury Lane

12 *Bermondsey*—London suburb

12 *Siddons*—Sarah Siddons (1755–1831), actress noted for
her tragic roles

13 *Reverend Johnson*—in *The Playmaker* Mary Brenham
is a servant to the Johnsons

14 *'Whilst there is life . . .'*—*Recruiting Officer*, II.ii.1

14 *the decree*—judgement

15 *copy the play*—Ralph wants Mary to make copies of
Farquhar's play for the other actors

15 *I read dreams*—in *The Playmaker* Dabby has a witch-
like ability to calm nightmares, notably Ralph's

15 *Play the flute*—perform sexually

16 *I'll look at it and let you know*—an ironic reversal of
the theatrical cliché whereby actors auditioning are let
down by the phrase 'We'll let you know'

17 *frippery, frittering, frigating, stricturing, contumelious,
flitty*—for comment on Ross's language see
Commentary p. xli

18 *Rousseau*—Jean Jacques Rousseau (1712–78), French
philosopher

20 *George Farquhar*—author of *The Recruiting Officer*,
see Background p. xviii

20 *Wilde*—a pun on the name of the Irish playwright,
Oscar Wilde

20 *Catholic doctrine*—Johnson represents the Church of
England. Transported Irish convicts were profoundly
Roman Catholic

20 *Grenadiers*—originally, soldiers who threw grenades

21 *sordid cohabitation*—many convicts lived together
without being married

22 *Before*—i.e. before having a sexual relationship

25 *willy-wally, wobbly, lewdy*—see Commentary p. xli

26 *Home Secretary*—the government minister responsible
for the law and, therefore, their presence in Australia

29 *I can bring a boat into any harbour*—Dabby Bryant became famous for a daring escape from Australia in a stolen boat. See Hughes p. 205

29 *ripe for the plucking*—ready to be seduced

30 *flux*—dysentery.

31 *'I have rested but indifferently . . .'*—*Recruiting Officer*, V.i.1

32 *'Welcome to town . . .'*—*Recruiting Officer*, I.ii.1

32 *heads of shires*—county towns

33 *Jack Ketch*—a name passed on to any public hangman

33 *Crap merchant, Crapping cull, Switcher, galler*—cant terms for hangman

33 *the Paddington frisk*—Tyburn was in the parish of Paddington – in dying the hanged victim danced the Paddington frisk

33 *noser*—spy, mole

33 *turn off*—hang

33 *whirligigs*—testicles

35 *myrrh, aloes, cinnamon*—fragrant aromatic spices

38 *'I would rather counsel . . .'*—*Recruiting Officer*, II.ii.60

39 *Johnson's dictionary*—Samuel Johnson's *Dictionary of the English Language* was published in 1755

40 *Latitudinarian*—one who favours latitude, freedom of opinion, especially in religious matters

41 *Screw jaws, Salt bitch*—cant terms of abuse meaning 'whore' and 'lecher'

42 *new wrinkles in your arse*—to have secret knowledge – Liz shows that she also knows of the escape of Kable and Arscott

43 *'None at present . . .'*—*Recruiting Officer*, I.i.137

44 *buzzed my wiper*—stolen my handkerchief

44 *wipe drawer*—handkerchief thief

44 *prigged*—stole

44 *rum diver*—clever pickpocket

46 *chic*—stylish

51 *thespists*—Ross's version of 'thespians', i.e. actors

53 *shifts its bob*—gets out of way

53 *ha'penny planet*—unlucky star

53   *nibbler*—petty thief
53   *crapped*—hanged
53   *titter*—daughter
53   *shoulder-clapped*—arrested
53   *prig*—stole
53   *trine for a make . . . wap for a winne*—why hang for a
      ha'penny when you can whore for a penny. Liz is
      advised to progress in the criminal underworld on the
      principle 'as well be hanged for a sheep as a lamb'
53   *dimber mort, swell mollisher*—beauty, good-looking
      woman
53   *mother of saints*—cunt
53   *swell cove*—gentleman
53   *bobcull*—good-natured fellow
53   *mossie face*—cunt
53   *shiners*—newly minted coins
53   *spice the swells*—rob the rich
53   *lifts*—steal
53   *stir my stumps*—run away
53   *squeaks beef*—gives the alarm
53   *snoozie*—a night constable
53   *nibbed*—arrested
53   *up the ladder to rest*—to be hanged
53   *fortune teller*—judge
53   *nap the King's pardon*—reprieved from hanging
53   *seven years across the herring pond*—Liz was sentenced
      to seven years' transportation
53   *rantum scantum*—sex
53   *nob it*—prosper
54   *rufflers*—rogues
55   *don't reach China*—Hughes (p. 203) mentions a
      paradise myth, held mostly by Irish convicts anxious to
      escape, that at a considerable distance to the north
      existed a large river, which separated this country from
      the back part of China, and that when it should be
      crossed they would find themselves among a copper-
      coloured people, who would treat them kindly
57   *Socrates*—(469–399 BC) Greek philosopher, the first to

apply serious critical and philosophical thought to questions of morality and the conduct of life

57   *Plato*—(429–347 BC) Greek philosopher, author of twenty-five 'dialogues', including *The Republic*

60   *dance the buttock ball*—copulate

60   *trull*—whore

65   *'What pleasures I may . . .'*—*Recruiting Officer*, V.iii.16

69   *'For I swear . . .'*—*Recruiting Officer*, II.i.56

71   *'Save ye, save ye . . .'*—*Recruiting Officer*, III.ii.145

72   *'The fellow dare not fight . . .'*—*Recruiting Officer*, III.ii.181

74   *'Captain, Sir, look . . .'*—*Recruiting Officer*, III.i.44

75   *'Yes, Sir, I understand . . .'*—*Recruiting Officer*, III.i.111

75   *canting*—the secret or peculiar language of a group, see p. xl

77   *'Captain Plume, I despise . . .'*—*Recruiting Officer*, IV.i.105

79–81   *pluming, muffy, gouly, ductile, possumy*—for comment on 'Ross-speak' see p. xli

81   *Et tu, Campbell*—ironic reference to Julius Caesar's last words ('Et tu, Brute'); Collins notes that even Campbell has succumbed to the influence of the play

84   *the circle*—upper level of a theatre auditorium

91   *'If any gentlemen soldiers . . .'*—*Recruiting Officer*, I.i.1